MILLION DOLLAR SOLOpreneur

MILLION DOLLAR SOLOpreneur

More Money. More Time. More Impact.

SANDEEP GUPTA

PENTAGON PRESS

Million Dollar Solopreneur
by Sandeep Gupta

First Published in 2014

ISBN 978-81-8274-796-8

To protect individual/institutional privacy, some names of people/places have been changed in the book.

Published by
PENTAGON PRESS
206, Peacock Lane, Shahpur Jat,
New Delhi-110049
Phones: 011-64706243, 26491568
Telefax: 011-26490600
email: rajan@pentagonpress.in
website: www.pentagonpress.in

Branch:
Prime Arcade
Office #11
1154 Saifee Street
Opp. M.G.Road, Camp
Pune-411001

Literary Consultant & Chief Editorial Coordinator:
Charushilla Narula (charushilla@outlook.com)

Photo Credit: Priyanka Dev

Printed at Aegean Offset Printers, Greater Noida

To all future Solopreneurs.

CONTENTS OF YOUR MILLION DOLLAR WALLET

WELCOME TO THE SOLOPRENEUR CLUB

Have you ever been insulted in public? Have you ever been treated unfairly? Can one five-minute incident change your life forever?

Foreplay

- At the age of 10, I was slapped on stage by a teacher in front of 500 people because I had forgotten my lines.

Intercourse

- I didn't go to school from the 6th to the 12th Std.
- I didn't go to college for seven out of eight semesters.
- For seven long years, I spoke to only three people – my parents and my mentor.
- I left home while I was at college.
- I worked as an auto-driver, a pizza-delivery boy, a porter, and even a construction worker on a daily wage of Rs. 50.

Orgasm

- I spoke as guest faculty at FMS Delhi before the age of 18.
- I successfully tried standup comedy.

- I interviewed more than 50 super-successful people and learnt their success-secrets.
- I read more than 3000 books spanning almost every discipline in the world.
- I dropped out of the best Business-School of Asia (IIMA) within a month of joining.
- I traveled to 37 countries spanning five continents.
- I rejected two of the most prestigious admission offers (MBA and Doctoral Programs) from Harvard.

Afterglow

I am a **Serial Solopreneur** and have created multiple businesses by running programs such as *Life Without A Boss, Your First Million Dollars, Million-Dollar Solopreneur, Know the World in 24 Hours, B.O.L.D.–Beware Of Lady Dynamites, The Jet-Set Speaker – Be the Millionaire Messenger, Your-First-Book, Own The Stage, Tri-Summit Storytelling System, C.Y.U.B.S. – Creating Your Unique Branded Solution, The I.M.P.A.C.T. Work Equation, The Laughter Lever, Universal Attraction Triggers, N.E.U.R.O.-Seduction, A.P.P.E.A.L. – Adorable Personal Positioning Exuded All Life, Pitch and Grow Rich Chronometer, Dynamic Delivery Devices, Kick-S.T.A.R.T. Content Creator, The 5C's of Engagement,* and *Stress-free Speaker S.Y.S.T.E.M.* I have helped more than 50,000 professionals live a life of their dreams. Thousands of my students have become Impact-Solopreneurs—Speakers, Authors, Seminar Leaders, Online Marketers, Video-Product Creators, and Consultants—and have attained *financial freedom for life*. All my programs have a unique promise—***more money, more time, more impact***.

In addition, my **Top-One-Percent** GMAT Training has helped thousands of students join ***Ivy-League Business Schools*** across the world. Whether at Harvard, Stanford, Wharton, Chicago Booth, Kellogg, MIT-Sloan, LBS, or INSEAD—my students can be found at each of these B-Schools.

OVER TO YOU

Commodity, anyone?

At the very outset, I have three questions for you:

- Do you want to make a lot more **money**?
- Do you want to do work that you **love** insanely, enjoy absolute **autonomy**, and have free **time** to enjoy your money?
- Do you want to create massive, direct, and tangible **impact** in people's lives?

I want to start with a bold claim: This book can make you wealthy, can give you more time and freedom, and can create more meaning in your life.

My boldest claim is: This book's lessons, if implemented correctly, can give you financial freedom for life in just the next 12 months.

You might snap: "A book can make me wealthy, happy, and free? Give me a break!"

But if you want to have a **Life without a Boss**, and want to be super-successful really soon, you have the tool in your hands to completely transform your life. The same tool has helped more than 50,000 people in the past to live a life of their dreams.

Think about this for a moment: If you want to impact people and create more than the 'normal' amount of wealth, the first thing you have to do is *stop exchanging your time for money*. There are two problems when you exchange your time for money:

- **You rarely reach a staggeringly high income:** For example, more than 99% people who are part of the corporate workforce in India earn less than Rs. 50 lakh per year. Now imagine if you conduct a two-day event, have 500 participants in it, and charge Rs. 20,000 per participant, you can make Rs. 1 crore in 2 days FLAT. That is Rs. 50 lakh per day!
- **A horrible limitation:** Even when you reach the top of the corporate ladder, you still have to put in hours to make money.

And there is such a horrible limitation to this equation. As of now, let's imagine that you put in 8 hours a day and make Rs. 1 (or 3) lakh per month, then by putting in, let's say, 16 hours a day, you may be able to make Rs. 2 (or 6) lakh per month. So this way, it is almost impossible to become a dollar-millionaire soon.

- o Now imagine that because you sell your products (videos/books), you don't have to move a single muscle to keep on earning. Your bank account keeps swelling even when you are sleeping/vacationing. How? Well, read on.

The first element in this absolutely fun-filled journey is to have complete autonomy (**Power**) over your own life. You need to have complete autonomy over the 4 T's – Task, Time, Technique, and Team.

According to the logic of autonomy:

- Only you should get to decide what you do.
- Only you should get to decide the time when you do whatever you love to do.
- Only you should get to decide how you do your work.
- Only you should get to decide whom you work with.

In effect, you have to be willing to **fire your own boss** first; in other words, you have to become a **Solopreneur**.

Imagine someone telling Picasso:

- You must paint this sort of picture.
- You must begin painting precisely at 8:45 A.M.
- You must paint it in this precise way.
- You must paint with the people we select to work with you.

Can you do *insanely great* work with such boundaries imposed on you? Let me ask you some questions upfront:

- Are you willing to **fire your own boss**?

- Are you willing to be an **Impact-Solopreneur**?
- Are you willing to live life amongst the **TOP-ONE-PERCENT**?

You are a Solopreneur if:

1. You are an IMPACT-Expert in a particular niche and sell your expertise through Professional Speaking, Writing (Authoring), Training, Consulting, or Premium Coaching.
2. You offer "live", "video", or "web-enabled" solutions that have the power to impact lives, businesses, and careers of your clients significantly.
3. You live your **life without a boss**. As a Solopreneur, you actually live *the dream-life* with:
   - NO BOSS
   - A minimalistic team, if at all
   - A significant IMPACT on people's lives, businesses, careers, relationships, health, or well-being
   - Freedom to choose your work
   - Complete autonomy over your time
   - Fame and prestige because of your expertise
   - A disproportionately huge income (imagine earning your current **monthly salary in a single hour** and enjoying loads of free time)—because I strongly believe *"If you are not earning enough, you are not serving enough!"* So my six-point motto for you is: (1) Be more, (2) Do more, (3) Gain more, (4) Enjoy more, (5) Esteem more, and (6) Give more.
4. You no longer have to exchange your time for money. You may be vacationing anywhere in the world but your products (videos/books/online products) will travel and keep making money for you even when you are sleeping (or vacationing)

So essentially a Solopreneur sells his/her skill, expertise, knowledge, advice, or wisdom; works alone, uses web/video technologies to reach out to the whole world; creates loads of money, time, and impact—without the typical trappings of an organization such as a boss, a team, or processes.

But you might think: "All this is fine, Sandeep, but your first point says that I have to be an **'impact-Expert'**. I am not an expert. I don't have any degrees or formal qualifications. Who will listen to me? What credentials do I have?"

Rest assured that these fears are not in isolation. Almost everyone asks me the same question. But this is the magic of this game: *you can become an Expert-Solopreneur overnight in virtually any field*. Let's understand this industry a little further.

THE 'EXPERT-SOLOPRENEUR INDUSTRY'

The Real *top-one-percent* Bracket

Haven't you sometimes wondered how some people out there end up being 'gurus' and highly-paid 'Experts', whereas you may know as much (or more!) and could do the same job (or better!)? But these experts are the perceived authorities in their respective fields, are the published faces of entire industries, and are well paid with money and attention.

What you may not know though is that there is no club to join, and no certification to pass, and **no degrees to be had** to be known as an 'Expert'. A weird and seemingly random collection of attributes can make our society believe and bestow upon you an 'Expert' tag. You can adorn yourself with the same attributes and BINGO! You're a de facto Expert!

What has driven the massive growth of this 'Expert-Solopreneur Industry' is the Internet and technological revolution that has allowed almost anyone to appear to be an expert. Joining the Expert-Solopreneur industry is especially easy, lucrative, and fast in any area in which you can sell information or information products, or any area that includes *speaking, writing, training, teaching, premium coaching, online marketing, or any other form of knowledge transfer.*

To start with, I present to you the **biggest myth-buster** in this entire book:

Expert positioning is not awarded; it is claimed.

So if you genuinely have the knowledge and skills to solve problems for people, you can claim your space in this Expert-Solopreneur industry and become the leader of a micro-tribe—and a micro-economy will be born. Join the industry and claim your space before someone else does so on your behalf. It is up to you and you alone to go out there, put your stake in the ground, and claim whatever is rightfully yours.

How to claim your expertise?

To understand this business of 'CLAIMING your expertise', let's meet some Solopreneurs of the modern era who sit at the very top of the pyramid:

THE AUTHOR: John Gray

John Gray is the #1 bestselling "relationships" author of all time. He is the author of over 20 books, including the best-selling relationship book of all time: *Men Are From Mars, Women Are From Venus*. His books have sold over 50 million copies in 50 different languages around the world. John is an internationally recognized expert in the field of relationships. For more than 35 years, John has conducted seminars for millions of participants. John is a popular speaker on the international speakers' circuit.

Food for thought:

- Who gave John Gray the tag of being the best RELATIONSHIPS expert in the world? **NO ONE.** He gave it to himself.
- Does he hold a degree/any formal qualifications in his **claimed** area of expertise? **NO**

THE ONLINE MARKETER: Jeb Blount

Jeb Blount is a sought-after speaker, trainer, professional sales coach, and the most downloaded sales expert in iTunes history. His Sales Gravy and Sales Guy audio programs have been downloaded more than 10 million times. In 2006, Jeb founded www.SalesGravy.com, a destination site for sales professionals, sales leaders, executives, and business owners, which has since become the most visited sales website in the world. He is the author of many books including the immensely popular book *People Buy You*.

Food for thought:

- Who gave Jeb Blount the tag of being the best Sales Expert in the world? **NO ONE.** He gave it to himself.
- Does he hold a degree/any formal qualifications in his **claimed** area of expertise? **NO**

THE SPEAKER: Anthony Robbins

The Solopreneur who has made the maximum money through SPEAKING in the history of this world: more than $200 million.

Tony Robbins is an American life coach, self-help author and motivational speaker. He became well known through his infomercials and self-help books, *Unlimited Power* and *Awaken the Giant Within*. Robbins writes about subjects such as health and energy, overcoming fears, building wealth, persuasive communication, and enhancing relationships.

Robbins' work has been featured in major media including *Time, Newsweek, Fortune, Forbes, Life, GQ, Vanity Fair, BusinessWeek, Tycoon, The Oprah Winfrey Show, SUCCESS* magazines, the *CBS Evening News, NBC News, ABC's Prime Time Live, Fox News, CNN A&E*, as well as newspapers, radio programs, and Internet media worldwide.

Robbins' programs have reached over 4 million people from 100 countries around the world. In 2007, he was named to Forbes magazine's "Celebrity" list. **Forbes estimated that Robbins earned approximately 30 million USD in that year.** In 2002, Robbins was ranked among the "Top Business Intellectuals in the World" by Accenture's Institute for Strategic Change. Robbins has spoken at

Harvard Business School and was ranked by the school among the "Top Business Gurus" (Harvard Business School Press, 2003).

Food for thought:

- Who gave Tony Robbins the tag of being the best Expert in the world in dozens of fields? **NO ONE.** He gave it to himself.
- Does he hold a degree/any formal qualifications in his **claimed** areas of expertise? **NO**

THE COACH: Patricia Fripp

Patricia Fripp is a keynote speaker, business presentation expert, sales presentation skills trainer, and an in-demand speech coach to executives and celebrity speakers. *Meetings & Conventions* magazine named her "One of the 10 most electrifying speakers in North America." She delivers high-energy, high-content, and dramatically memorable presentations. *Kiplinger's Personal Finance* identified *Patricia Fripp Speaking School* as one of the best ways you can invest in your career.

Fortune 500 companies maximize their investment by engaging Patricia for keynotes, breakout sessions, and to coach their executives on their presentations. Patricia is known for simplifying and demystifying the process of designing and delivering powerful keynote speeches and sales presentations. Patricia is the successful author or coauthor of these great books: *Get What You Want, Make It, So You Don't Have to Fake It, Speaking Secrets of the Masters, Speaker's Edge,* and *Insights into Excellence.*

Food for thought:

- Who gave Patricia Fripp the tag of being the best Presentations Skills Trainer in the world? **NO ONE**. She gave it to herself.
- Does she hold a degree/any formal qualifications in her **claimed** area of expertise? **NO**

My question: What is common among these Experts-Solopreneurs?

The Answer: None of them holds a formal qualification in the topics that they speak about. Nobody gave these people a tag, an honor, a degree to go and charm the world. Nobody gave John Gray any permission to become the best relationships-expert in the world. All these people simply CLAIMED their topics. In fact, Tony Robbins used to work as a janitor and Patricia Fripp used to work as a hairstylist before these people CLAIMED their respective topics.

Among the many topics that I have claimed in the past, *"The Only Corporate Storytelling Expert in India"* needs a special mention. Even though I don't have any formal qualifications in 'storytelling', nobody has asked me for any proof. I am offered a standard Rupees one lakh per hour and more than 100 Storytelling engagements come my way every year.

So stop falling into this negative self-talk again and again:

- What qualifications do I have to claim a particular topic?
- Who will listen to me?
- I am so young. So inexperienced. So ugly... why will people pay me to listen to me?

I have successfully claimed the following topics in the past without any resistance:

- India's only Solopreneurship Expert
- India's only Expert for Professional Speaking on Global Stages
- India's only Corporate Storytelling Expert
- The most blasphemous GMAT trainer on this planet
- Asia's only Neuro-Marketing Expert

One of the best examples of this "claiming" idea is my program *"Know the World in 24 Hours"*. By its very name, people should doubt this program; on the contrary, this has been one of the most successful programs to have ever been run by me. Nobody has come back to me saying: "How can you claim something like this?" No one has ever asked me as to how I could make them know the whole world in just 24 hours!

What helps you claim your topic?

- **An IMPACT/SERVE/TEACH mindset**: The strong belief that although you are an ordinary person, you definitely have a message, a process, a piece of advice, a skill, an expertise, a story, or some specialized knowledge that can significantly impact/ change other people's lives, businesses, careers, relationships, and/or health. So you want to share what you have learnt and shorten people's learning curve. If you took 5-10-20 years of trial-and-error to learn how to do something and now can package that learning in a way that people can learn from you in a very short amount of time, you will find it very easy to claim your topic.

- **Your convictions/your personal belief system:** When you have a strong conviction that your solution can change something significantly for people, you will do everything within your power to claim your topic and to get your solution across to them.
- **Your life-story/your personal journey:** If you have overcome some major obstacle in life, you will have a huge amount of belief in claiming your topic and offering your solution. You must strongly believe in these tenets:
  - "My life story, my knowledge, and my message—what I know from experience and want to share with the world—have a great importance and market-value."
  - "I am here to make a difference in this world, and the best way to do so is to use my knowledge and experience (on any topic, in any industry) to help others succeed."
  - "I can get paid for sharing my advice that helps others succeed, and, in the process, I can build a very lucrative business and a profoundly meaningful life."
- **If you have already got some RESULTS** in your life, you can share your success-secrets with people and help them get the same results by sharing with them the same process that you followed. In this case, it will be extremely easy for you to claim your topic.

Again, remember that you don't need any degrees or formal qualifications here. All you need is one or more of the aforementioned points.

THE 'EXPERT-SOLOPRENEUR GRAPH'

Fact: Do you know that only **0.17%** of people in the world are dollar-millionaires? (Approximately 12 million out of approximately 7 billion people), so financially speaking, if you are a dollar-millionaire, you automatically belong to the **top-one-percent** people in the world.*

The Twist in the Tale

In any industry, only a handful of people make bulk of the money.

From Hollywood actors to chefs, and from pop music stars to football champs, there are only a few who make the big money, while the rest just get by. Let's understand this by the graph and the table below:

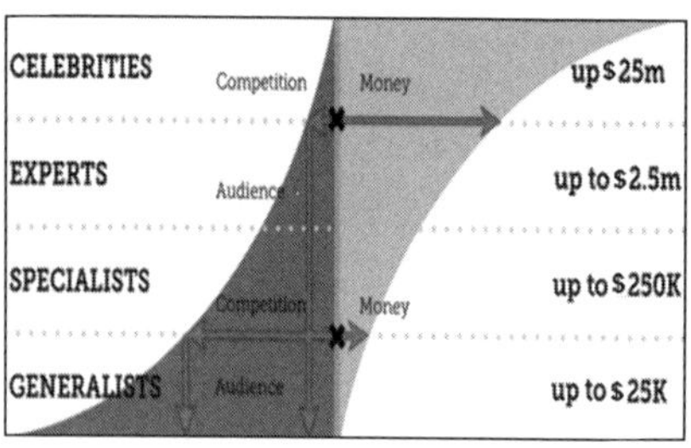

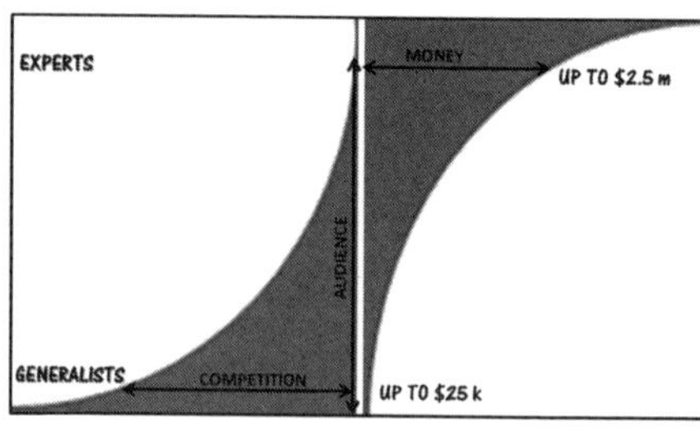

Individual	Money	Money Ratio	Characteristics
Celebrities	Up $25mn	1000X	
Experts	Up to $2.5mn	100X	Very little competition, huge audience, mega bucks
Specialists	Up to $250K	10X	
Generalists	Up to $25K	1X	Big competition, small audience, little money

I repeat: In any field, market, or industry, most people are perceived to know very little about a topic, and a very small number of people are perceived to know a lot.

Source: http://en.wikipedia.org/wiki/Millionaire#Number_of_millionaires_in_the_world

Please notice that I have used the words **'perceived to know'**, not **'know'**. The reason is that the way we look at the position of a person on the matrix is pretty much exclusively based on their **expert status**, not their true knowledge or ability to perform a certain task. A small number of people get the 'big money', while a majority of them have to fight for scraps.

Let's look at **Sameer**, a health coach who is passionate and knowledgeable about nutrition and who helps people with their diet. Sameer loves what he does and he is good at it. He knows his stuff. But he is not perceived as an expert among many people. If you were to put him on the graph, he would only find himself at the bottom 5%.

There are three problems with Sameer's positioning.

- There are hundreds of thousands of people positioned where he is, making Sameer a 'Generalist'.
- Because of his position, Sameer can't reach many people (his audience) and can therefore help very few people.
- The money available in the marketplace for that level of position will keep Sameer struggling to survive, creating potential resentment, and might ultimately result in Sameer not enjoying what he does.

On the contrary, if you belong to the top of the positioning axis, you have pretty much NO competition. At this level, your personality becomes more important than your work. I can illustrate this with an example of a celebrity chef in India. Do you think Sanjeev Kapoor is really in competition? Is his ability to 'make food' actually that important?

Instead his style, personality, values, and mission make him what he is today. This allows him to move into the 'Celebrity' segment of the matrix, where he can form and lead tribes and sell pretty much anything with his name written on it.

Can YOU become a Well Paid 'Expert-Solopreneur'?

I am always asked this question: WHO can benefit from this kind of positioning? After 18 years of Solopreneurship across Industries and domains, and after helping more than 50,000 people with my Solopreneur Blueprint, I can safely say that this formula can be applied to virtually any industry.

I have personally seen miraculous results in: Motivation, Attitude, Success Secrets, Relationships, Leadership, Spirituality, Stock-Investing, Style and Fashion, Business Growth, Productivity (time management etc.), People Management (teamwork etc.), Health, Fitness, Wellness, Marketing, Branding, Digital Marketing, Social Media, Sales, Persuasion, Parenting, Entrepreneurship, Solopreneurship, Brain Science, Storytelling, Knowledge, Perspectives, Design Thinking, Meditation, Web Design, Renovation, Real-Estate Investment, Digital Product Creation, Nutrition, Public Speaking, Presentation Skills, Professional Speaking, Singing, Dancing, Acting, Comedy, Business Coaching, Body Transformation, Life Coaching, Pet Grooming, Hair Dressing, Accounting, Publishing—the list is long—and possibly endless.

Why should you become an Expert-Solopreneur?

My definition of an Expert-Solopreneur includes teaching and leading people. I don't want to think of Experts as scientists or nerds being locked away in some lab or in front of a computer. My Experts are people who love people and who go out to spread the word. AND you can simply **claim** your Expert-Solopreneurship Positioning without waiting for anyone to reward it to you.

Because no one ever will!

Here are my reasons why you must become an Expert-Solopreneur:

1. **Make more MONEY in less TIME**: There is literally no glass ceiling on how much you can earn in the Expert-Solopreneur industry. Your pay equals the value you deliver, not the hours you work. As an Expert-Solopreneur, your income can outpace the income in absolutely any other industry.

2. **Do what you love and get paid for it:** If you establish your **Expert-Solopreneur** positioning, then life can indeed be a breeze. Life's too short to waste it on something you hate doing. As an Expert-Solopreneur, your work is based entirely on your passion and knowledge; your activities essentially include 'relating to people' (speaking/writing/consulting) and 'creating' (your talks/your books/your seminars/your products).
   - In addition, you can work anywhere/anytime, you can work with whom you want, you barely need a team, and the tools for success are exceptionally simple and ridiculously cheap.
3. **"Get CHOSEN" instead of "keep CHASING":** Imagine yourself going from door to door offering your product or service. This is what most people do. Now imagine people coming to you because you are the go-to person in the industry. Which role is more fun and more rewarding? Once you are an Expert, people will find you. Business will come to you, not the other way round.
4. **Become a Leader in your industry:** Experts are de-facto leaders. And it is more fun leading than following. Let's face it: you either lead or follow. You either play or watch. And from all the evidence I have observed, leaders get paid and get the glory; followers ... well, follow. And only one percent of all the people in the world are leaders; the remaining 99 percent people are followers. As a successful Expert-Solopreneur, You have a great chance to belong to the **top one percent** people in the world.
   - Have you ever seen one listener and 100 speakers? Speakers LEAD; listeners follow.
5. **Design your future lifestyle:** As you enjoy absolute autonomy over your task, time, technique, and team, you have the liberty to design your future lifestyle and choose your working model. There are three possibilities here:
   - **Full access mode:** you are always needed to take care of your business. Not a great idea.

- **Mixed access mode:** you conduct a few big events/trainings/workshops, but most of the times you sell your products (books/videos). This is what most Solopreneurs follow.
- **No access mode:** you sell only your products (books/videos)

6. **Chuck what you don't want to do:** This is an extremely crucial element in choosing your future lifestyle. What precisely do you not want to do? For example, I don't like to be a part of any day-to-day operations. I believe in creating (my content) and relating (to a group), but there are dozens of small operational aspects of my business that I don't like to carry out myself. You need to figure out what doesn't make your heart sing and avoid that work.
7. **You have a choice**: Do you want your business to be based on your skills or on your personal story? Needless to say, story-based Solopreneurs (such as Tony Robbins) are much more – may be a thousand times more – successful than skill based Solopreneurs (lawyers, accountants, or math teachers). I have used both the models, but nothing beats a personal story-based model. For example, my programs Life without a Boss, Million-Dollar Solopreneur, Know the World in 24 Hours, The Jet-Set Speaker, N.E.U.R.O.-Seduction etc. are story-based offerings. But my GMAT training program is a skill-based venture. You need to decide upfront whether you want to be a story-based or a skill-based Solopreneur.
8. **Now is the time:** For a Solopreneur, I consider YouTube/Video Hosting the biggest boon of the modern era. Imagine this: just 10-15 years ago, if a Corporate Speaker/Trainer had to come out with a promotional DVD to be sent to promoters/companies/HR, they would have needed the following steps:
   - Hire a recording studio/hotel
   - Make sure that sound is captured perfectly with the video
   - Get the video professionally edited (sleek with titles, proper cuts, zoom-ins etc.)

- Physically distribute/courier the DVDs to various parties
- Wait for months for their responses

The list can go on. But this meant that only those with deep pockets could have done this.

Now imagine this:

- You can get HD quality video from your iPhone/webcam of your computer.
- You can get perfect audio quality with a small microphone inserted into your computer.
- You can edit the video at absolutely no cost (so many free video-editing programs are available for you to choose from).
- You can upload the video on YouTube and just send a link to the interested parties.
    - YouTube is the second biggest Search engine in the world after Google. And if you have a video, your rank on Google search goes up significantly.
    - In fact, the new economy can easily be called the VIDEO economy.
- Interested people can instantly watch the video on their smartphones or other mobile devices.
- You can offer secure online video products (Since October 2012, I have bought video subscription products worth more than Rs. 50 lakhs).
- If you wish to offer physical media, you can encrypt the videos to the level of non-copiable access on one computer only. You can also include an expiry date (all this at virtually no cost).

Money, independence, freedom, and purpose are some of the ingredients of the Solopreneur life. And if you apply the ideas from this book to your business and life, you'll have more money and more time available to spend on the things you love.

I know what you are thinking: "all this is fine Sandeep, but HOW—precisely HOW—does it all happen?"

THE SOLOPRENEUR BLUEPRINT

After having a thorough understanding the WHY and the WHAT of the entire concept of Million Dollar Solopreneur, it is time to deep-dive into the HOW. I present to you my entire Solopreneur model, **The Solopreneur Blueprint**. The beauty of this Blueprint lies in its entirety, its integrity. Miss one piece and you miss the whole Millionaire-dream by miles. The Blueprint is a staircase; the order of the seven steps is extremely important. You can't skip any step or change the order. So read this entire book in the exact sequence. The exact Blueprint is shown on next page.

Against each step, the names of the programs/courses/sessions that I offer as **live** sessions and **video** products have been mentioned.

In the subsequent chapters, you will learn about these steps in detail, one by one. Time to deep-dive!

The first step in your Solopreneurship journey is your story: your Personal Journey (fueled by Passion and Purpose). In the first chapter, I present to you my story – my personal journey.

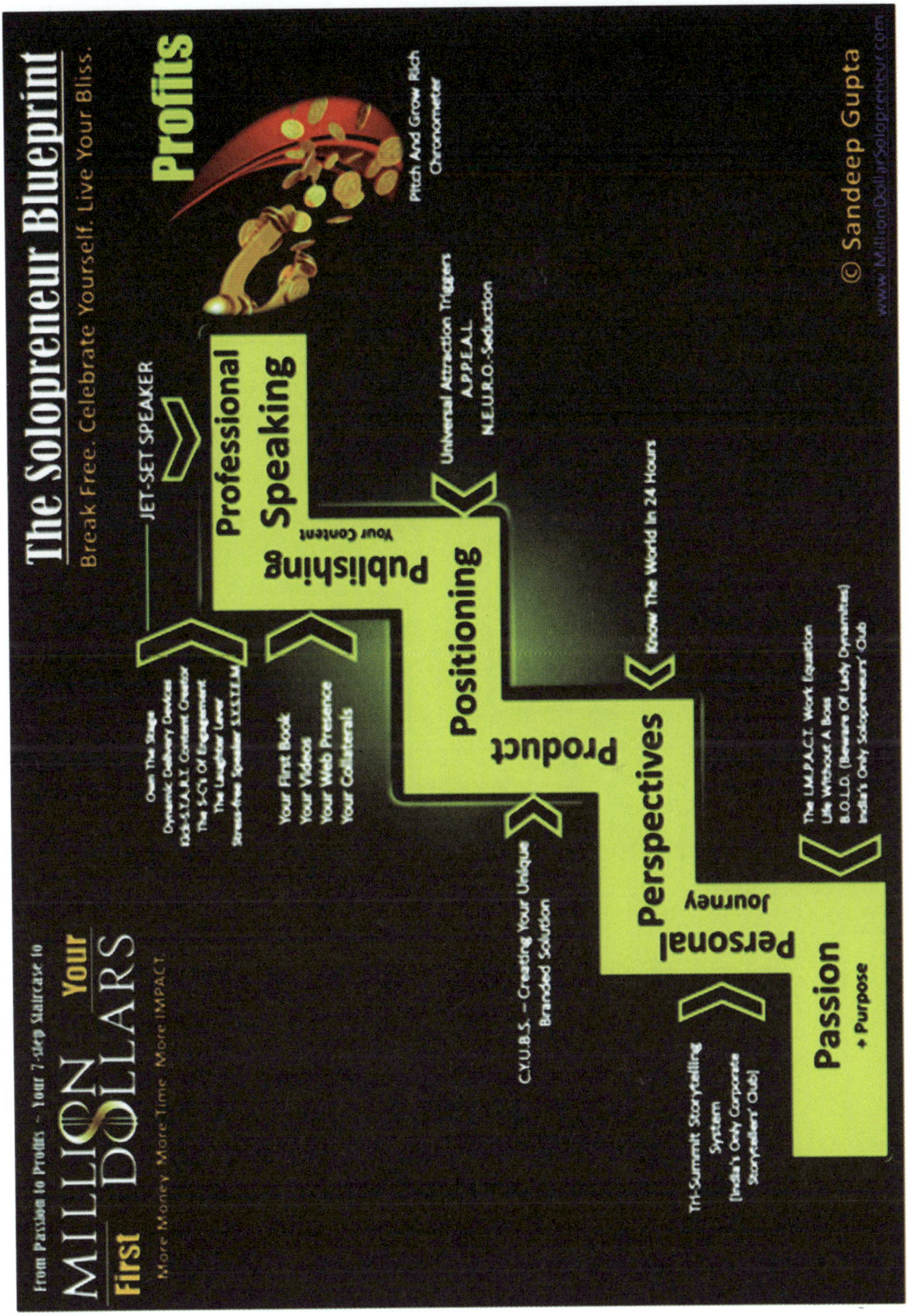
From Passion to Profits ~ Your 7-step Staircase to
First MILLION Your DOLLARS
More Money. More Time. More IMPACT.
The Solopreneur Blueprint
Break Free. Celebrate Yourself. Live Your Bliss.
Profits
Pitch And Grow Rich Chronometer
JET-SET SPEAKER
Professional Speaking
Publishing Your Content
Positioning
Product
Perspectives
Personal Journey
Passion + Purpose
Own The Stage
Dynamic Delivery Devices
Kick-S.T.A.R.T. Content Creator
The 5-C's Of Engagement
The Laughter Lever
Stress-Free Speaker S.Y.S.T.E.M.
Your First Book
Your Videos
Your Web Presence
Your Collaterals
Universal Attraction Triggers
A.P.P.E.A.L.
N.E.U.R.O.-Seduction
Know The World In 24 Hours
C.Y.U.B.S. – Creating Your Unique Branded Solution
The I.M.P.A.C.T. Work Equation
Life Without A Boss
B.O.L.D. (Beware Of Lady Dynamites)
India's Only Solopreneurs' Club
Tri-Summit Storytelling System
(India's Only Corporate Storytellers' Club)
© Sandeep Gupta
www.MillionDollarSolopreneur.com

$

PERSONAL JOURNEY

Fueled by Passion and Purpose

Dad, will you Kill Mr. Bhatti and go to Jail?

Have you ever been treated unfairly? Have you ever been insulted in public? Can just one five-minute incident change your life forever?

The tussle: I come from a Delhi-based family of Civil Servants (both my parents were civil servants). Curiously enough, my family epitomized a very modern lifestyle coupled with an equally regressive outlook towards life—truckloads of ill-gotten money, luxury brands, foreign trips, club-memberships, insistence on the right knife & fork, impeccable social-standing, swank house (felt more like a prison), farmhouse-parties, an army of domestic-servants, imported cars—the lot. All that life meant to them was 'beating others' in the social pecking-order. But they were stuck in a time-warp when it came to having different or unique opinions. They found even laughing at themselves scandalous. I am sure that, throughout their working lives, my parents never consciously thought about having a positive impact on even one person. They were just mouthpieces of the government and the society around them. I never found them having any original or fresh ideas. Among their peer group, meeting one person was the same as meeting all of them. No one had any fresh perspectives on life. Consequently, life was extremely boring during my early years. *Perhaps this explains why (throughout my life) I have always craved the company of people who were unique in some way: passionate, rebellious, liberated, witty, iconoclastic, defiant, politically-incorrect, controversial, free-willed—the lot.* I was always fascinated by the unknown because the known was really boring. I just wanted to break free from the prison. But the more I tried to speak to people, the more 'stuck' I found them.

The turning point of my life: I was born on 28th June, 1974. In my family, right from an early age, 'reading' and 'speaking' were encouraged. When I was in the 5th Std., I got my first opportunity to speak on stage. It was for the school's annual day. My parents were really excited. We (children) were to stage a small play based on a story of human, spirit, and tiger. I was chosen as the narrator as I had a clear voice. Our Arts (Drawing, Dramatics, and Fine Arts) teacher Mr. Satinder Bhatti had prepared us for 2 weeks.

At about 40, Mr. Bhatti, a tall and slender man, had an impeccable sartorial elegance (looked quite like Navjot Singh Sidhu). He was a perfectionist. He would lose his temper even while dealing with ten-year-olds who didn't even know what performing on stage actually meant. Oddly enough, I had been a victim of his slapping many times in the past. He put us through a grinding two-week practice. He relented only when he was doubly sure that there would be no screw-ups on stage.

Finally the day arrived—the day I won't forget all my life. We all reached backstage and were anxiously waiting. Ours was the third group. I tried to peek at the audience of more than 500 people from behind the stage. It looked jam-packed with people—parents, teachers, the school principal, and the chief guest.

If you had been sitting in the audience, you would have witnessed something that you would have never forgotten all your life. At our turn, the compère announced: "Please welcome 5th C with their brilliant play." The audience gave us kids a huge round of applause. As the narrator, I had to start.

I started: "Good afternoon to all of you." Just at this very moment, there was a sound of an electrical fault: I heard a 'booommm' sound and saw some sparks on the background wall. Suddenly my mind was off the script. I blanked out. Completely! The entire auditorium went "SHHHHHHH!!!" And then the crowd went into a whispering mode.

Mr. Bhatti came up on stage, looked down at me with threatening gestures and blurted: "SPEAK!!!" Suddenly he snatched the mike from my hand and told the audience, "I apologize for this. We will start in just a minute."

He started shouting: "SPEAK!!!! What are you waiting for?"

When I couldn't recollect my lines, he started:

> "It is useless to teach you. You can't remember even four lines. My dog is better than you. He can learn in one shot."

Suddenly, in front of 500+ people, he went into an overdrive of abuses in Hindi and Punjabi. I looked up, staring at him in disbelief.

Again he went: *"Kya, ghoor kya raha hai?"* He slapped me and pushed me so hard that I fell on the stage.

"Never come on stage in your lifetime. *Zindagi mein bhool se bhi kabhi apna muh mat kholna."*

I had failed in my first-ever public appearance—in front of 500+ students, parents, teachers, and the chief guest. But to me, the failure didn't mean anything. What got to me was the insult. He had insulted me in front of 500+ people.

I was ANGRY! And I was HURT!

> *The insult was so intense that all I wanted to do was prove Mr. Bhatti wrong. But, strangely, I was torn between two absolutely conflicting emotions: the intense desire to speak on stage again*

versus the fear of failing again. Except for my parents and BD (following his request, I am not at liberty to disclose the name of this gentleman), *I barely remember speaking to anyone at all. For seven years, I didn't go to school. Deep inside, the desire to prove Mr. Bhatti wrong still kept simmering from time to time but the FEAR kept winning.*

As they say, "everything happens for a reason" and "you can connect the dots only looking backwards" ... today I feel extremely fortunate to have experienced such an incident early in life.

At that moment, the chief guest Mr. BD (coincidentally, he was a junior colleague/friend of my father) stood up and went on stage. He said, "This was a barbaric treatment. Teachers are supposed to encourage students. I promise you Mr. Bhatti. I know this boy and his family. This boy will come back and speak better than any of your students. I will train him personally and show you. From today, he is going to be my student."

Seething within, Mr. Bhatti left the stage without saying anything.

My father went up to the principal furiously (he has always been hot-tempered) and shouted:

> *"Mujhe Bhatti chahiye!!!Abhi!!! Main uska sar fod doonga!!! Bhale hi mujhe jail ho jaaye!!!"*

The principal went up on stage and apologized for the unfortunate incident. The event was called off.

I ran up to my parents and all I kept on saying was: "I won't ever go to school. Teachers are bad people."

My exams were approaching. With great reluctance, I wrote the exams. During that time, BD came to our house frequently. He convinced my parents that I needed to divert my attention. My parents trusted BD blindly.

After the exams, once summer vacations started, BD took me to his place for 2 weeks. He took me to the movies/superstores/libraries etc. He asked me to forget it all. I would promise: "YES. I won't ever talk about it." And after 10 minutes, I would again ask innocently: "Will Dad really kill Mr. Bhatti and go to jail?"

BD told me a story about how he had been ditched by his girlfriend and how he had spent many months of his life totally devastated. He had become totally negative, filled with hatred for the girl. Finally he read an article by Shakti Gawain, which had a line: "Nobody ever died of a snake-bite. People die of venom." This statement had such a profound impact on him that he forgave the girl and, since that day, had achieved remarkable successes in life. He tried to explain the same to me. It was not Mr. Bhatti's words but the hatred for the man that was killing me. He wanted me to read that article, so he took me to a library where he had spent many years reading and preparing some of his best works. He told me: "Whenever I am in Delhi, I spend at least 4 hours each day in this library."

My parents thought that this phase would pass and that I would soon forget all about the incident. But I was clear: "I won't go to school." I liked BD's company so much (ironically, he was 29 and I was 10) that I wanted to meet him daily. BD developed in me the habit of reading to obsessional levels. Every evening he would tell me the book I was supposed to read the next day, give me the summary of the book beforehand, and pique my curiosity to the level that I couldn't wait to get started with the book. My driver would drop me off at the library at 11 am. Each day, I would read the book that BD had asked me to, and, when he would arrive in the evening, he would give me more wisdom about the same book. He would fill all the learning gaps and suggest the next book. Three months of summer vacation were spent like this.

One thing that **no other person** could have taught me: **the ability to connect the dots.** I will give you one example to explain how he gave me this ability. Initially just to divert my attention, BD took me to some movies, superstores, and libraries. During one such visit to a Superstore, he picked up a Nestlé chocolate and this is how the conversation went:

BD: "What is this?"

Me: "A chocolate."

BD: "Tell me more."

Me: "Nestlé is quite yummy. My favorite."

BD: "MORE!"

Me: "I don't know."

BD: "Read the wrapper fully. What do you find?"

Me: ......

BD: "I asked you something."

Me: ......

BD: "Which country is it from?"

Me: "I am not sure."

BD: "It is given on the wrapper?"

Me: "Oh yes! Switzerland."

BD: "What do you know about Switzerland?"

Me: "Ya! You told me that *Silsila* (the movie that we had watched a few days ago) was shot there."

BD: "*(almost pulling his hair)* What else do you know about it?"

Me: "NOTHING!"

BD: "Where is Switzerland?"

Me: "I don't know. But I don't think it is in India."

BD: "It is in Western Europe."

Me: "OK!"

BD: *(fuming)* "I expect a question."

Me: "What question?"

BD: *(shouting)* "I said, 'Western Europe.'"

Me: "So?"

BD: "If I say 'Western Europe', how is it possible that the question *'Western!? So there must be something called Eastern Europe, otherwise why give it the name 'Western'?* not come to your mind? Where is your focus?"

Me: "I never thought of it."

BD: "There is a big division in the world these days because of this. You have to know this."

Me: "OK!"

BD: "This is not a physical division but an ideological division. The world is ideologically divided into two parts."

Me: "What is ideological?"

BD: "Based on belief, thought, idea. Not based on borders. See! You live in the same house but you don't like some things your parents say, right? So it is not a physical division, but an ideological one. Imagine you have a brother and a sister. If your sister supports your stand if your brother sides with your parents, it will not create any physical divide but an ideological one. The world calls it the Cold War."

Me: "So who are the two sides here?"

...

BD gave me the **most fascinating account** of the entire history of the last 70 years (from 1914 to 1984), WW-I, WW-II, The League Of Nations, The Treaty of Versailles, Hitler's rise to power, The Bipolar World, The Division of Germany, The Berlin Wall, The Cold War, The Formation of UN, Communism, Capitalism, The Russian Revolution, The Formation of China & Taiwan, The Formation of Israel, Arab-Israel conflict, the Iron Curtain, the Cuban Missile Crisis, the Afghanistan Crisis, US versus USSR, the Arms Race, The Yom-Kippur War, The Oil Shocks of 1973 and 1979, OPEC and its role ... PLUS ... at least a hundred more such stories.

Which other teacher in the world can connect a Nestlé wrapper to such a fascinating account of world history?

Just to give you one more example of what a great mentor can do for you:

On another day, he picked up a Coca Cola bottle (it used to be an imported product then), he asked me similar questions.

BD: "What is this?"

Me: "Coca Cola! Should I read the bottle fully?"

BD: *(nodded)*

Me: "Atlanta, GA. What's GA?"

BD: "It is Georgia."

Me: "Oh! The country near Russia you told me about?"

BD: "No! This Georgia is different."

Me: "You mean there are two Georgias?"

BD: "YES! This one is in the US."

Me: "How can two places have the same name? If I say, I am going to Georgia, how will you know which one?"

BD: *(big grin on his face)* "You have a lot to learn. OK! What else do you know about Coca Cola?"

Me: "It is good but *thoda teekha hota hai*."

BD: "I mean The Coca Cola Company."

Me: "I wonder what they put in this drink."

BD: "It is the biggest brand in the world."

Me: "What is a brand?"

BD: "OK! If I ask you about butter, what comes to your mind?"

Me: "Amul. I love *paranthas* with it."

BD: "Exactly! So Amul is a brand. It is a big brand because it comes to your mind first when you think of butter."

Me: "So, 'brand' means 'famous'?"

BD: Not exactly! But, in a way, you can say so."

Me: "So Coca Cola is so famous?"

BD: "Yes! It is sold in more than 100 countries around the world, and the symbol of 'Coca Cola' is the most recognized word in the English Language. Even when Russia and America are enemies, Coca Cola is sold inside the Russian Parliament. That's why the Coca Cola logo is considered the symbol of the victory of capitalism around the world."

Me: "REALLY! How did it become so big?"

BD: "The power of Positioning."

Me: "Means!"

Then BD gave me the entire history of Coca Cola's success. How a small pharmaceutical brand (started in 1886, about a hundred years ago) that used to contain cocaine earlier went on to become a massive brand fascinated me no end. He told three things that amuse me even till date:

1. The fact that the design of the Coca Cola bottle was inspired by a woman's skirt (the 'hobble-skirt' design) intrigued me no end.
2. The fact that there is nothing secret about the Coke formula but the company has always publicized it as such. It says that Coca Cola has a secret magic formula that is hidden in two parts of Trust Bank's locker in the US. The two top executives of the company know only half the formula each. That's why they don't travel together on the same plane (this is a myth created by the company).
3. The fact about how Coca Cola was made the official free drink of all American soldiers during the Second World War, an action that resulted in making the company truly global. It had to open bottling plants wherever the American army went, especially all over Europe, automatically making the brand truly global. He also told me about how American soldiers (who were the winners of the war) got a celebrity status in the US in the 1940s. Since the soldiers drank Coke (because they had been addicted to this "free" drink) and the people in the US wanted to emulate their war heroes, they also started drinking Coca Cola as a symbol of victory. This is how sugared water was positioned to become the number one brand in the world.

BD used to tell me dozens of such stories every day.

Why would you want to go to the boring school after such fascinating lessons?

Once July approached, my parents raised the issue of school again.

And I threw the same lines: "No school! No teachers!" I held my ground. "Even if you kill me, I won't go to school."

BD explained to my parents: "Let him take his time. For the time being, enroll him in a school where attendance is not compulsory. Give me six months. I will fix the issue."

Finally, my parents enrolled me in a shady school. To them this was the biggest anticlimax – my elder sister studied in an International School and I was enrolled in a school that didn't even bother about attendance.

The strangest thing: BD secretly admired me for having stood my ground in front of my parents. To me, this was quite SHOCKING. He showed me two quotes from Vivekananda:

> "Take up one idea. Make that one idea your life—think of it, dream of it, and live that idea. Let the brain, muscles, nerves, and every part of your body be full of that idea and just leave every other idea alone. Consult your heart, not others, and then follow its dictates. Let it be so great, so strong, that there may be nothing else left in the mind; no place for anything else, no time for anything else. Whenever we attain a higher vision, the lower vision disappears of itself. This is the way to success."

This quote sums up passion, focus, perseverance, excellence, vision, mission, purpose, and boldness.

> "Each great work has to pass through three stages—ridicule, opposition, and then acceptance. Those who think ahead of their time are sure to be misunderstood. Have you got the will to surmount mountain-high obstructions? If the whole world stands against you—sword in hand—would you still dare to do what you think is right?"

This quote sums up REBELLION – fearlessness – the readiness to change the world.

As an example, he told me the story of Raja Ram Mohan Roy. He asked me: "When that man (more than a century ago) could stand against the entire world for championing causes as rebellious as abolition of the Sati system, idol worship, child marriage, caste-system etc., you can surely do exactly what your heart says is correct. **Rebellion is the name of the game**. Not going to school doesn't mean a bad life. Face your parents (and the whole world) with the utmost rebellion if you think what you are doing is right. NO MATTER WHAT HAPPENS, always follow your heart."

Nothing could have been more coincidental. Earlier in the same year, Apple had unveiled its most historic campaign – the Macintosh. BD showed me a recent issue of *The Economist* with the cover having pictures of Bill Gates and Steve Jobs. It read: "Will dropouts rule this world?"

He told me their stories in detail. While talking about Steve Jobs, he also drifted into the Objectivist approach to life. He spoke about Howard Roark in *The Fountainhead* and about Dagny Taggart and John Galt in *Atlas Shrugged*. He also shared the story of Ayn Rand (how she had moved from Russia to America and her entire philosophy). Finally I was convinced that formal education had nothing to do with high-stakes life-success.

He gave me a success formula to evaluate whatever I was to do in life later:

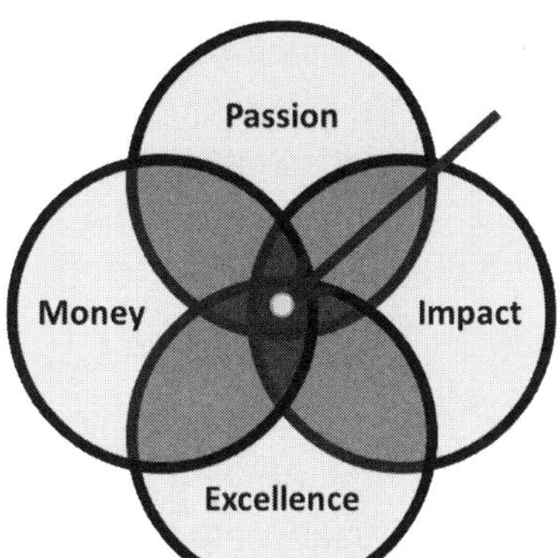

Passion: Are you insanely passionate about your work? Are you able to transmit your passion and positive energy to others?

Impact: Are you impacting people, lives, careers, businesses etc. in a big way? Are you creating immense value for the people/world? Are you impacting lives, careers, businesses, relationships directly?

Excellence: Are you the "best-in-their-world"? Are you in the top-one-percent (excellence) in your domain?

Money: Do you make satisfactory money?

The answer is a thumping 'NO' for almost all of us.

Imagine what the world will be if the answer to all the questions above could be a huge 'YES!'

I wanted such a life for myself – at the intersection of all the four circles. From that day onwards, PASSION and REBELLION have been my watchwords for life.

Things settled a bit back home as my parents gradually calmed down. All this while, once a week, I had a personal tutor at home who would teach me all the school subjects. Apparently, I topped the school in the annual exam of 6th Std. (Imagine the level of the school! I scored 47% and still topped). This was my biggest bargaining counter with my parents. I finally told them: "I will write the exams but won't go to school even in 7th Std." Apparently, they had no choice but to reluctantly acquiesce.

> One of the best things that happened: all the three people around me encouraged the habit of reading. And I took a fancy to it. In the absence of school (that would have gobbled up 8-10 hours each day receiving useless knowledge that makes no sense when it comes to success in life), I was receiving life-success lessons from a super-achiever-genius-maverick. At 30, BD epitomized success like nobody else. This Economic Advisor to many Governments was extremely well-read, personified Howard Roark, and was a maverick professor (an author, a brilliant speaker, and enjoyed many other accolades).

I celebrated the fact that I didn't have to go to school: I had enough time to just dig myself into books and read for hours on end. Practical life-success lessons from the most successful people in the world were handed out to me in the form of absolutely fascinating stories. ON A PLATTER! And thus started my life's biggest love-affair—an affair with books—that continues unabated till date. I relished every single book I read. I could read and understand these books because BD used to give me a complete backdrop about each book before asking me to read it.

> The books/publications that left the biggest impression on me: The Harvard Business Review, The Economist, Pirates of the Valley, The Fountainhead, Atlas Shrugged, Positioning, Cosmos, The Dragons of Eden, Future Shock, Power Shift, Third Wave, Bertrand Russell's Philosophy Collection (35 books), and all the books by Tom Peters. Each of these books was absolutely elevating. With the passage of each book, I felt even more 'enriched' and 'ready'.

As I read more and more complex stuff, I faced two problems: poor vocabulary and low reading speed through tough texts. I got so bugged by my poor vocabulary that I bought The Oxford Advanced Learners' Dictionary and, in the next six months, remembered it almost fully with the proper usage of each word. My problem of vocabulary was solved, once and for all.

To fix the problem of slow comprehension, BD suggested that I gain a basic idea about most of the basic human disciplines: business, economics, marketing, biology, history, evolution, paleontology, anthropology, philosophy, psychology, astronomy, literature, science & technology the works. This was a catch-22. To learn these disciplines, I had to comprehend tough texts fast. And to comprehend fast, I had to know these disciplines.

BD suggested a different approach. He enrolled me into a video library. It contained a huge collection of documentaries on almost every subject on this planet. As per BD's suggestion, I would rent one video-cassette per day and watch it fully. Also, he suggested watching all the foreign programs on TV. It took me a few years but I must say that I have never made a better investment in my life.

> Watching British comedies on TV was an extraordinary investment. Apart from humor, I learnt about global politics,

the roots of the European crisis, investment banking, and a zillion other disciplines from 'Yes Minister', about the retail industry/customer service from 'Are You Being Served/ Fawlty Towers', about WW-II and the last hundred years of world history from 'Allo Allo', about complete 360 degree shades of human psychology from 'Porridge' etc. Also, the documentaries proved extremely useful. For Instance, imagine watching a three-hour documentary on The Kalahari Desert. No geography or science book can match that learning. I ended up watching more than 500 documentaries on almost every subject in the world. THE BEST INVESTMENT OF MY LIFE! Reading became a cakewalk after this investment. My overdrive with books had catapulted into the highest orbit. Between 14 and 18 years of age, I read more than 200 books per year on almost all disciplines.

I loved BD's reason for making reading the ultimate hobby: I can't still forget what he once told me when I asked "WHY READING?"

BD's answer: "Someone who has written a good nonfiction book must have been a good reader. Now let's say this person had read 100 good books before planning to write one. Obviously they would have wanted to put their best learnings into the first book. So in effect, this person would have tried to give you the wisdom of at least a hundred great books in their book. So if you read one great book, you indirectly receive the wisdom of at least a hundred great books automatically."

Since then, reading has been my all-time-favorite hobby. It feels magical. Getting into the mind of someone who has radically different perspectives on the world is sheer adrenaline, kick-starting my brain to connect disparate dots of information to make a symphonic meaning. Reading the work of someone who is more knowledgeable, more skillful, and more accomplished gives me ecstatic exhilaration. I can spend countless hours with great books.

But I couldn't talk to anyone. It was not shyness. It was fear. The more I tried to speak, the more I would go deeper into my world of books/documentaries/TV/writing.

My biggest blow came when, in 1990, BD left the country for a few years on an assignment. I felt devastated. It was like losing my parent. He was everything to me: friend, philosopher, guide, mentor, and coach. The only guiding force in my life was gone.

In BD's absence, my parents got a grip on my weird ways and asked me to apply for Engineering. I have no clue why I listened to them and complied. In 1991, I finished my XII, and joined Engineering (in July 1991).

College was a complete disaster; it was as if I had come from a different planet. Prior to college, for seven long years, I had forgotten things such as classes, teachers, friends, teamwork, bullying, gossip ... the lot. I found it very difficult to adjust.

I failed every single subject in my first semester (this must have been a record in the history of the college). As per the rules of the college, I was expelled for six months. Strangely, I felt really good and relieved. I thought I wouldn't have to come to college, after all. One good thing did happen, though: I made a friend, my classmate Sarang—my first breakthrough in seven years.

In January 1992, Sarang once called me over to his place. While we were chatting, I heard a huge debate going on in the other room. I was fascinated and just walked into the other room. Sarang's father and one of his friends were discussing the issue of oil prices. Both of them were professors at the Faculty of Management Studies (FMS), the best business-school in Delhi.

IMAGINE ... can your destiny change in a single moment? FOREVER!!

I have no clue what came over me in that moment.

While they were blaming liberalization (that the government had recently initiated in 1991) for the high cost of oil, I unwittingly said:

BLAME HITLER FOR THE HIGH PRICE OF OIL.

[This line ... just one legendary line...changed my destiny. Completely!!! Seven years spent with books and documentaries conspired together to change my destiny in a single moment.]

Turning to me, both of them reacted as if I was eating spiders. Sarang's dad (Prof. RM – *like the other gentleman, this person also requested me not to share his name*) said, "Sandeep, do you realize what you just said? *Tumhari tabeeyat to theek hai*? How is Hitler related to this mess that the Indian Government has created?"

And I explained the entire thing:

> Hitler—Concentration Camps—Genocide—persecution of Jews—Jews fleeing to Jerusalem in millions—formation of the UN in 1945—formation of Israel in 1948—raw deal to the Palestinian Arabs—US/UN favor to Israel—Israel, the fighting nation—simultaneous fighting on five borders and winning—US direct support to Israel in the Yom Kippur War of 1973—Arabs angry—Oil Embargo on the Western world by OPEC (predominantly Arabs)—Oil Crisis—Oil Shock of 1973—prices increased to 6 times the base price within one year—no rollback on prices since then—the base changed from X to 6X—the entire humanity is still paying a huge price for Hitler's atrocities.

These two gentlemen, along with Sarang, were completely engrossed, leaning on my each word with absolutely rapt attention. Once I finished, after a long silence, RM spoke: "Sandeep, I am amazed. Where did you learn all this? I am a B-School professor and I keep interacting with the smartest people in this country, but I haven't ever heard anything as fascinating, not even remotely as fascinating, as this." *(Hinting to the other professor) "What do you think?"*

The other professor said, "RM can be possibly excused because he is a professor of Marketing. But I teach Economics. And I must confess: I am feeling as if I know nothing about the subject. You should come to the college and share this with our students. I am serious. In 18 years of my teaching career, I am yet to hear a more interesting insight."

Both of them wanted to know more about me. I told them about the books, documentaries, and my extreme interest in at least a dozen disciplines.

That day, I had a six-hour long discussion with two of the sharpest people in the city of Delhi. I spoke about almost all the disciplines I had been exposed to. To me, what I spoke wasn't important. It wasn't important that they were impressed. The only important thing was that I could speak for hours to two strangers. You may not be able to empathize here because you probably can't imagine how big a victory this was for me. Seven and a half years of "clamming-up" and the pain that had accompanied that feeling all along the line—all the trauma—was suddenly gone. It was as if I had been released from a dark-prison cell after many years.

This was clearly my day – the happiest day of my life.

RM called me over the next day and asked me to address the students at the college.

Picture this for a second: You are reminded of the most horrendous past and are asked to re-live it!!!

I froze dead in my tracks! "NO!! Over my dead body! I can't speak in public." And he was puzzled. "WHY???" I told him the entire Mr. Bhatti episode. I told him that the mere mention of 'speaking to a group' completely 'throws' me.

He counseled me: "See, yesterday you spoke to three people. Could you have spoken if Sarang's mother, your parents, and two mores professors also had been present?" I said, "Yes." He convinced me that if I could speak to eight people, I could speak to eighty people as well. He promised me: "I will make sure that you will speak extremely effectively in front of the group. Even if it takes months of training, I am ready to train you personally." He even called up my parents and told them the same. They couldn't have been more ecstatic.

And thus began my training sessions! For the next two and a half months, every single day, I practiced and delivered as per RM's instructions. He never made me feel like a junior student, someone he was helping to tide over a problem. I felt more comfortable in his presence than in Sarang's or BD's or my parents'. This man had something magnetic about him. He could make me feel like an equal, like a million dollars. Apart from the training, we would discuss marketing, branding, positioning, and ad campaigns. Almost daily he would say, "Kotler sucks", and would get a chuckle from me. On March 29 I told him, "I think I am ready to go on stage."

The stage was set. He had publicized me so much that everyone was looking forward to some gems of wisdom from this genius child-prodigy. The audience was about 125 people (including my parents). I was the youngest person in the room. I was supposed to speak for 15-20 minutes. As I was introduced, I heard a deafening applause. As I had been trained, I started: "Imagine if the book **Das Kapital** had not been written, what would have the world been like?" Well, just to encourage me, some professors responded: X, Y, Z would have happened. But the perspective I gave shook the students completely. I received applause after applause.

Now I know that initially they applauded just to encourage a 17 year old. But after 15 minutes their applause turned genuine. The content was completely unheard of by them – breathtakingly fresh perspectives on the current global economic, political, and military scenario, positioning, branding, psychology, triune model of the human brain, entrepreneurship and almost all that I had learnt in so many years. I was unstoppable. It was as if someone had opened the floodgates of an overflowing dam. I left the audience completely mesmerized by my content. My delivery was extremely raw but the content alone had the power to completely spellbind them. The 20-minute session went on for more than 200 minutes. They were lapping it up. And I was completely unstoppable. As the speech came to a close, RM asked the audience, "Should this boy come for more such sessions?" Everyone said, "YEEESSSSSS!!!" **This was my moment of reckoning.**

Till date, I don't think I have had a happier day. Both my parents were jubilant. I hadn't seen them this happy earlier. Their 'worthless' son had achieved something after all. My parents told RM: "You did the unthinkable. You should get an award." And RM said something that I have never forgotten: ***"I have never reached for a trophy. I have always reached for a life."*** During that conversation with my parents RM showed them a card with three quotes. He said that his life was personified in these three sentences:

> "Your true worth is determined by how much more you give in value than you take in payment."
>
> "Your influence is determined by how abundantly you place other people's interests first."
>
> "The most valuable gift you can offer someone is yourself."

WHAT A PERSON! I wonder about these lines all the time, and continue to apply them in my businesses.

RM deserved all the credit for the spectacle that I had achieved. Why would anyone sacrifice three months of his own life to remove my fear of speaking? He had nothing to gain. Still he went out of his way to help me so much. I couldn't have believed such a story if anyone else had told me the same. I would have discarded it as an OTT movie-script. On the one hand, there was Mr. Bhatti, who could spoil someone's life in just five minutes, and on the other, there was Prof RM who could give the same person his life back. He also rekindled my Harvard-dream, something that had been forgotten after BD had left. "You deserve to go to Harvard", said a proud RM. The impact of this man on my persona was indelible. From an introverted-fearful, I was becoming an extrovert-fearless.

That day, I decided to be a trainer, a coach, a guide. My future was chosen in a moment. I didn't know what to do or how to achieve my goal. But I had to impact lives. I had to touch lives. It felt as if this is what I had been sent to do on this planet.

In the meanwhile, Sarang (who was a regular in his second semester) told me that the HOD of our department had threatened that it was compulsory to attend his tuitions to pass irrespective of preparedness levels. If you didn't pay him, no matter how good you were, you would fail. If you paid him, you would pass, even if you were to leave the answer-book blank. You had to study only if you wanted to get great marks. In order to pass, you had to just pay him and forget about everything, including attendance. You didn't have to go and attend his tuition classes, either. *Talk about the fairness of the system*!!

My second innings at college was sensational. As Sarang had made my speaking triumph public, I was hailed as a celebrity among students. I also made four very close friends (Bhavna, the daughter of an extremely successful entrepreneur, Anil – from an army background, Rohit – a US based NRI, and Vikram – a UK based NRI). All of us shared a common interest: extremely diverse reading. None of us attended a single class from the 2nd to the 8th semester.

For one year, all five of us did nothing except sit outside the classes daily and talk for hours on dozens of issues. Each discussion was a heated debate, with none of us ready to concede an inch. Truly electric and edifying! On most days, the debates would continue well past college hours. Every day, we would go back with a feeling of having learnt something significant. Life couldn't have been better.

But this was college; back home another incident once again changed the course of my life forever. My father had a colleague who had always been an extremely honest civil servant throughout his career. He and my father were part of an assignment together. The entire operation reeked of extreme irregularities, malpractices, and corruption, and virtually everyone in the government was neck-deep in this morass. Somebody blew the whistle and the case came up for hearing in the Tribunal. The two officers were questioned. Despite knowing that his colleague was absolutely honest, my father sided with the government, an action that *de facto* proved his colleague dishonest. My father sided with corruption as he too was neck-deep into all wrong practices himself. This honest officer was found 'guilty' and was suspended from the Service. He couldn't bear this stigma and hanged himself. At that time, the government virtually owned the media. The news was hushed and never caught any public attention. **But this jolted me. COMPLETELY!**

I developed an extremely strong antipathy towards this whole system that my parents were part of (painfully, my mother also sided with my father). I raised hell. Absolute hell! How could my father live in peace after what he had done? He had (virtually) murdered a colleague. It was never clear to me as to why such talented people as my parents had to resort to corruption. They could have chosen any career for themselves. They could surely have been honest and held their heads high. But to no avail. There were counter-arguments in the house trying to convince me: "You can't be copybook-honest; honesty only brings you the sidelines. Honest people are crushed under the feet."

This was completely unacceptable to me. It was unimaginable for me to live under the same roof. I was disgusted beyond redemption. I wrote a note and just left home.

Enter the real-world! From the silver-spoon, velvet-glove world to 'the streets' in a matter of hours! For the next one month, I lived with an old servant of ours who had started driving an auto-rickshaw after leaving our house. He lived with all sorts of workers. I didn't tell anyone what I was doing or where I was, but, out of a sense of loyalty, this servant of ours told my parents about my whereabouts despite my strong resistance. But I could easily ward off their sympathy. For the next one month, I did everything I could just to sustain myself. I waited tables, delivered pizzas, drove auto-rickshaws, ported trolleys (at the airport), and even moved bricks at construction sites.

I loved it all. Absolutely! During one such pizza-delivery, as a kid opened the door, I saw XI Std. Physics and Mathematics books lying on the shoe-rack. And I unwittingly rattled off the entire syllabus. The kid couldn't believe his ears. He sighed: "*Bhaiya, aap ko yeh sab* *kaise aata hai?"* and I said: "I am doing engineering." He looked completely lost (he was preparing for engineering himself). He called his parents and told them the same. They asked me to come in and showed some curiosity. I told them my story. They were completely bowled over by my knowledge of English and Math. They asked me something completely unexpected: "Could you teach Varun (the son) Mathematics? We are anyway looking for a tutor. We can pay you Rs. 100 per hour (the standard rate for tutors in Delhi then)." **HUNDRED RUPEES AN HOUR?**

I wasn't making that much money even by working for the entire day. I immediately agreed. As per Varun, I did an extremely good job of teaching Math and he drummed up the news among all his friends. Soon I was teaching 12 of Varun's friends in a group. Seeing this, a local training center hired me to teach Mathematics on a '50-50-sharing-basis' to the students of XI/XII/Engineering Entrance Tests. This center had hundreds of students. Soon I was making up to Rs. 35,000 per month (which was more than my parents' combined official salary at that time).

BACK TO COLLEGE: All four of my friends were aiming to write the CAT (the Common Admission Test) and go to the IIMs. But I was smitten by Harvard. Strangely, till just a few years ago, Harvard accepted candidates without work-experience. I wrote the GMAT and got a perfect 800/800. There was no counselor in Delhi. So I went to Mumbai to meet the most renowned study-abroad consultant in India. This guy fumed looking at my ignorance. "What kind of a student are you? What homework have you done? Don't you know that work-experience is compulsory for HBS? And you have written the GMAT and nurtured your HBS dream without knowing this basic fact? And you have even traveled to Mumbai to meet me? I am appalled at your abject ignorance of basic facts." He sent me back with a truckload of fleas in my ear. **I felt SHATTERED!!!**

But whom could I have blamed except myself? I didn't have a clue in the world as to what to do next? I met RM and he suggested that I consider the IIMs instead. Around the same time, Bhavna shared an incident from Shashi Tharoor's life, detailing how he had spent a full year when he was 12. He made it a point to read one book a day and to finish exactly 365 books in a year. And he did finish 365 books. This was indeed inspirational. Bhavna and I decided to read one book each daily and discuss it in the evening. Both of us joined a library and finished 608 carefully chosen books (together) in 365 days. Although our target was 730 books combined, we still felt thrilled to have accumulated the knowledge/wisdom of 608 books in one year.

In the meanwhile, I also became receptive to the idea of the IIMs and the CAT. I joined a CAT Training institute for its test series and topped in three consecutive mock tests. The chairman of the company called me and offered me a very well-paying job. Because I wanted to get into training, I thought everything around me was conspiring to take me there. I immediately said yes. The job gave me a 360-degree exposure to the functioning of a large Education Company. I never sat for any on-campus placement at college. I was clear: "When my ultimate goal is to become a trainer, why work in a company that is not into Education and Training?"

The experience came in extremely handy when I ran my own businesses. I was exposed to some of the most fascinating situations when I worked in Sales under our National Sales Head. On my first day in Sales, I faced a life-threatening situation (a man with a gun!) but negotiated it really well.

Once this company called Barry John (the leading acting and dramatics coach in India) to conduct a one-day training workshop for trainers. I was extremely fascinated by his entire approach and joined his school in Noida for a month-long training. The results were spectacular. Someone at his school suggested that I try standup comedy (this, according to him, was the best solution to remove any inhibitions from anyone's personality). I read a few books on standup comedy (Judy Carter's book was clearly the best) and prepared my own content. I had already developed quite a few funny bones, thanks to my friend Anil (the wittiest person I have ever met). His sarcasm, wit, satire, insults, and puns were exemplary.

Anil made me rehearse for my first show, a mere 15 minutes. It came out 'ok' but not great. He helped me tweak my content and delivery. Finally I thought of just diving in front of a live audience.

I volunteered to do my shows free-of-cost at the swankiest club in Delhi (I had been a waiter here before, so I used some contacts to get the entry). The who's who of the city were part of this really posh place. With deep skepticism, they allowed me 15 minutes. After getting good feedback, I got to do the shows every Friday. I became quite popular during this time. I did 14 consecutive weekly shows spanning 3 months.

When I told RM about my standup comedy, he suggested something really unusual. He asked me to approach these successful people and just ask for 15 minutes of their time. He even gave me the lines that I used with each of them.

"Hello Sir/Ma'am, I am just starting out in my life. You are so successful. I request you to give me just 15 minutes of your time and tell me what I should do to become as successful as you?" I asked 62 people and all of them agreed. I could finally talk to 51 of them. I interviewed Entrepreneurs, Entertainers, Artists, Politicians, Bureaucrats, Authors, Sportspersons, Musicians—all sorts of successful people. My objective was to understand the PSYCHOLOGY of success and winning. One more thing happened as a result of interviewing these people: I could talk to any stranger in the world. I became a true extrovert. The learnings from these people proved more valuable than what the top 10 MBAs in the world combined could have taught me. Absolutely crucial life-success lessons were handed out to me on a platter.

One thing that was common to all these people was: PASSION. They were passionate to a fault about what they did. An irrational internal drive (*Junoon*) for what they chose to do was manifest in each of them.

***

I often wonder: "How many people go through life in such kaleidoscopic colors by the age of 22?" For most people, life till 22 means school, college, classes, exams, studies, parties, gossip, relationships, sports, movies, music, dance, and finally a decent-paying job that they love to hate.

I wrote the CAT and made it to IIMA. I thought this would be an end to my roller-coaster life. But it wasn't to be. **Life had extremely exciting plans in store for me.**

In the first week itself, I was disenchanted with everything at IIMA – a place where not an iota of real entrepreneurship was ever talked about. I wanted to run away.

Something inside me wanted to revolt. People told me that this was the stupidest idea that they had ever heard in their lives. I persisted amidst the cacophony of dissenting voices from friends, peers, seniors, faculty, administration—everyone.

I learnt one important lesson that day: ***The biggest battle in the world is the battle inside your own mind when you have to take a really BOLD decision.***

What Catalyzed my Decision?

1. The wisdom gained from 51 successful people. Nothing that would be taught in a two-year MBA at IIMA matched the success-lessons that I had learnt from these people.

2. At IIMA, for one day, you could sit in any of the second-year classroom sessions and decide your electives in advance. I sat in the 'Entrepreneurship' class that was offered as an elective in the second year. It was ATROCIOUS. Imagine a professor who had never seen the outside world (had never even worked for a company as an employee, let alone been an entrepreneur) teaching you the theoretical concepts about entrepreneurship! Could anything else be a worse learning experience?

3. I didn't like anything—people, peers, faculty—nothing. I hated the idea of grades. For instance, could the guy who topped the quiz/exam in Economics actually contribute to

the Macroeconomic policy of the country better than the rest of the class could? I had a day-long discussion with him and he admitted to knowing nothing about the complexity of national-policy decisions. But he had the biggest tag to back it: IIMA's Economics topper.

4. What was the point of a tag if it didn't enable one to sell even a packet of Nirma better than the guy who had spent some time on the field selling it? If the purpose of life was to make mindless Spreadsheet(s) or PowerPoint(s), I didn't want to be a part of the bandwagon. I wanted to impact people directly.
5. **The quote:** "Each great work has to pass through three stages—ridicule, opposition, and then acceptance. Those who think ahead of their time are sure to be misunderstood. Have you got the will to surmount mountain-high obstructions? If the whole world stands against you—sword in hand—would you still dare to do what you think is right?"

Finally I did the unthinkable. I put up a formal application to leave the school. This was my moment of decision. And as Tony Robbins says:

> IT IS IN YOUR MOMENTS OF DECISIONS THAT YOUR DESTINY IS SHAPED!!!

That day, for the first time, I could fully relate to this quote. My destiny indeed got shaped in this moment of decision. I was ecstatic that I could finally take such a bold decision.

Starting July 1996, for the next three years, I ran my first Solopreneurship venture (a CAT, GMAT, and GRE Training Center) at Ahmedabad. I did really well by every stretch of the imagination. In less than 3 years, I trained 3357 students, produced scintillating results, shaped careers, impacted lives, and saved enough (despite my extremely wild spending habits in those days) to easily afford a 5-year career-break. At this juncture, I desperately wanted to travel the world.

For the record: After the first year in business, I visited my old school, gave the Principal a cheque of Rs. 100,000 as donation, and spoke on the school stage as a successful entrepreneur. Life had come full circle for me. After I told the Principal about the barbaric treatment at the hands of Mr. Bhatti, the Principal called Mr. Bhatti and introduced him to me and left the room. I told Mr. Bhatti the entire story of my life. He remembered the incident perfectly well. He was profusely apologetic. I just said: "THANK YOU SIR! Without your insult, I wouldn't have been the person I am today." That day, I felt a sense of unprecedented calm.

I sold my center to the franchisee of another CAT-Training company and, in turn, got a handsome golden-handshake for giving the franchisee a competition-free market and an extremely booming center from day-one.

In the meanwhile, I got addicted to investing. The thrill of the stock-market was just insane; it made me a true adrenaline-junkie. I did well on numerous occasions, but lost all the money when I once traded in oil derivatives. All the money was gone in a single day.

I had to earn to survive even for the next month. After a lot of effort, through some referral, I managed to get a job (I happened to join the dotcom bandwagon). I joined Britannica as Chief Content Officer for its India Operations. I excelled in my work from day one. My reading habit of more than a decade paid off handsomely. I won seven excellence awards in seven months. I shot through the ranks and was shifted to London. Though I was probably earning much more than I could have dreamt of in any job, I still felt a void within. I just wanted to travel the world. One day, as part of compulsory training offered by the company, I attended a conference – *The Future of Emerging Markets* – at the London Business School. This event, too, prompted a 'moment of decision'.

A part of me wanted to resign immediately but somehow I wasn't fully sure. My boss made every attempt to retain me, to the extent of tripling my salary and offering me a stake in the company + ESOP. As he ratcheted up the stakes, the decision to leave got tougher and tougher. Although I had realized that I wasn't meant to work for a company or a boss ever in my life, somehow this decision wasn't easy for me. I discussed this with a friend and she called me an idiot to even contemplate refusing the offer my boss had made. I even cried that day – my first in more than a decade. The next day, the same friend called me up and said: "You are so smitten by the new idea that nothing will be able to keep you at your present company. No matter how hard your boss tries to retain you and whatever salary he offers, just go for your dream. "**YOUR DREAM IS NOT FOR SALE.**"

F*CK!!! What a profound statement this was! This one line meant the world to me. Quitting was painless after this. The next day, I QUIT, without feeling an iota of fear, guilt, or remorse, and came back to India. I got really hooked to the idea of Emerging Markets. I could mix business with travel. I took a formal online course in Emerging Markets and just loved the excitement this field had to offer. I started my second entrepreneurial venture, and in the next four years, I got the opportunity to travel all around the world.

****

One of my biggest failures: I completely misread a person – failed to understand her completely. Love and loss!

The root of the problem was that whenever I met a person, I would somehow convey (implicitly or explicitly) that I was not interested in knowing their past, especially the messy, sad, or sloppy details. Whenever I met people, life was all about laughter, fun, and wit. I never shared my past, either. This habit culminated into a perfect copybook instance of "love and loss".

When I started working on emerging markets, my first assignment was with a UK-based Lifestyle Company that wanted to foray into emerging markets, especially Asian markets. The assignment was challenging and I loved every moment of it. I needed to hire someone who would have worked in lifestyle, fashion, retail, and marketing. In September 2000, through some referral, I hired a partner, Kanika. She was extremely rebellious, feisty, and passionate—my perfect match. We worked together on some of the most wonderful projects and traveled the world on our assignments. We planned a vacation together in Hawaii if we were to crack Rs. 1 crore in 3 months. She worked endless hours making presentations, plans, pitches and the whole gamut of consulting shenanigans. 24x7, life was absolute fun; we just worked hard and partied harder. I handled the content and she handled the operations.

We clicked like a house on fire. She became my most intimate partner. Soon it turned into an intense relationship. She gave her 100% to both her work and our relationship. Our conversations were always intelligent, funny, and witty. We would sit together and talk in puns for hours; it was so much fun – so much fun – that the darker side never surfaced.

We went to the US to crack a deal with an online-content company that was looking to develop channel partners in India and other Asian markets, and decided to move straight to Hawaii after the deal. While we were staying at the Ritz-Carlton, she happened to ask me, "I barely know about your childhood." And I told her the story of my failure on stage and the entire trauma that I had undergone for seven long years. And I just happened to say, "You can't imagine what I went through." **This was the turning point.**

She started crying. She told me that I had no idea of what she had gone through. She revealed that she had had a really bad past. As a youngster, she had been abused by some men in her family.

This is one thing I can't stand! No matter what! Such people should be lynched and hanged in public.

The next few weeks were extremely traumatic.

The next day, I pacified her, left her at the hotel, and went to meet the client. When I came back, I found that she had slit her wrist at three places and had to be hospitalized. For the first time, I saw so much blood—a white bed-sheet completely bloodstained. I reached the hospital and found that she had gone into acute depression. You would have heard the doctor say: "Sandeep, this is a vital blow. She ain't getting fine soon."

I was devastated. I really cursed myself for never tapping into her world. For a few days, I couldn't sleep even a wink. After a couple of days, when she regained her senses, she told me that she had always been receiving psychiatric treatment, had had a history of chronic drug (substance) abuse since the age of 16, and had a very tough relationship with her family.

For the first time in my life, I felt helpless. Nothing worked for about 20 days. She was under acute depression. In the meanwhile, I made the final presentation to the client and bombed miserably. We lost the client at that very moment. In such a state, traveling back home wasn't possible. She could go violent anytime. And her violent phases were extremely ugly. So much so that she could pick up a knife and kill herself or anyone in front of her.

I couldn't sleep much, and on one such sleepless night I watched Anthony Robbins' infomercial. He claimed to cure depression in just 5 minutes. This caught my fancy. I had heard all great things about Tony Robbins and I found that this could be the best hope for an otherwise miserable life. He was going to do his next event in Florida after seven days.

So if you had been with me, you would have been sitting in the front row (reserved for the victims and their attendants) at the Orange County Convention Center in Florida.

Robbins is a great guy. Just superb! He breaks your pattern. If you have been sad, he would ask you about the time when you were happy. If you are suffering from a disease, he would ask the time when you felt the healthiest in your life. At about 12:30, he called her out.

So she's on the stage in front of 5000 people. And Robbins asks her: "what makes you so unhappy?"

She starts crying, re-living her horrendous past.

And I am feeling miserable. I am cursing myself to have come here. And suddenly Robbins breaks her pattern.

He asks: "have you ever had an explosive orgasm?"

She goes *"haaan…* ???" with a strangely quizzical look on her face.

That's a change of state. She goes from depression to a different state that is not depression any more.

She says, "Yes."

Robbins asks, "Could you describe how it felt? Could you re-live that experience?"

She is like: "I can't do that." So he asks 5000 people in the room, "Can she tell us about her experience?" And everyone goes "YAAYYYY."

And she starts telling the entire peaking experience in "When-Harry-Met-Sally" style. And I am wondering, "What's happening?"

****

She became all fine. In a matter of five minutes, he changed her life. That evening, I saw my partner back to life, absolutely springing back to the feisty Kanika that I had known. It was as if every bad experience had been deleted from her memory.

Next day, Robbins asked: "what would you dare to do if you knew you couldn't fail?" Whoa! What a profound statement!

I couldn't sleep that night. I remembered a similar statement Jim Collins asks in his book *Good to Great*: "If you have 20 million dollars in the bank and just 10 years to live, what would you dare to do? Do that NOW."

Looking at Robbins, I thought: "look at the positive impact you can have by being a Professional Speaker. You can change lives." I decided: "I will change people's lives. Even if I can change one life, it will be worth the effort." I decided to be a professional speaker and make people more knowledgeable, entrepreneurial, and BOLD. I have always been indebted to the most impactful person I have ever seen in my life: TONY ROBBINS.

And I was not alone. Tony left such an impact on Kanika that even she wanted to be a Professional Speaker and help people. We just needed to wrap up a few assignments in India. She didn't want me to wait to start. So we decided that I would stay in the US to get trained on Professional Speaking while she would handle the company in India for a few months to wrap up all the unfinished work as soon as possible. Every day we would exchange messages/ calls just to talk about one thing: speaking and impacting people.

I started to look for avenues to get into professional speaking in the US. After a huge effort, I got one speaking engagement, and I screwed it up royally! And seriously I needed help.

I found out (by extensive research) that Patricia Fripp was the best Professional Speaking coach in the world.

> I called her and said, "Ms. Fripp, I would like to be coached by you."
>
> She asked, "Are you sure?"
>
> I said, "Yes! I have done my research, AND you are the absolute best."
>
> She asked, "Do you know how much I charge?"
>
> I said, "It doesn't matter."
>
> She said, "It is a good attitude. That will be $14,000 per day."

("*I am pretty happy with the skills I have.*")

So many times we see the price of doing something but we don't see the cost of not doing it.

She said, "Perhaps you are not ready yet."

I asked, "Could you evaluate one of my speeches and accordingly tell me how much training I will need?"

I thought, "She would find me okay and I would need to change me a bit here and there."

I sent her the video. And she called me, "Sandeep, I have gone through your video, AND ... Darling! You need me. If money is a concern, come and join one of my workshops that charges $4000."

So I spent $4000 attending her single-day workshop in Vegas. I realized that I knew nothing – ABSOLUTELY NOTHING – about Professional Speaking.

That day I learnt a very important lesson in life: Although I was good, I couldn't be complacent with what I had – learning never stops. I was not even one percent compared to her. ***What got me here won't get me there.***

****

Kanika was completely fine for quite some time. We would exchange mails/call each other multiple times each day and nurture our Professional Speaking dream.

She took to drugs again and developed meningitis. This claimed her life.

I had no clue of any of these ghastly developments. I couldn't get through to her for many days. Her phone was always unreachable. I didn't know any of her family members/ acquaintances. This made me almost delirious. I had absolutely no idea as to what was going on. I called my clients and office assistant but nobody seemed to care. Frantically, I packed my stuff and boarded the next flight to India. Still, nobody seemed to have a freakin' clue.

I kept dialing her number like a mad man but to no avail. After 12 days, someone picked up. It was her elder brother. It emerged that she was no more. And he narrated what had happened.

> "One day, she ended up having a massive argument with dad and completely lost control. She went back to the same mess that had almost finished her life: drugs. She overdid it and developed severe meningitis. Within 12 hours, she was no more."

I was so blank that you could have knocked me down with a feather! The whole world had been slammed shut on me.

The next few months were really hard. Eventually I could somehow reconcile to the inevitable loss but one thing kept on haunting me and **I needed some answers**. Even after six months, I couldn't get over **WHY** she did what she did. Why do we behave so irrationally? Why do we do things that make no sense? Why can we not control our behavior? Why can we not behave rationally?

I read almost everything about human behavior but almost all of it seemed like complete ***psychobabble***—totally unconvincing. Just one book made some sense. It was the only book that talked about the role of the human brain/evolution in human behavior. Finally, there was light at the end of the tunnel, lots of it. As I surfed/read more on Brain Science, Evolutionary Neurobiology, Cognitive Sciences, Triune Model of the brain—The Triune works, everything started to make complete sense. The concept of the Triune Model of the brain is so powerful and intriguing that it leaves you completely 'fulfilled' with all the answers. I finally got all my answers. And I was raring to share this with the world.

My professional speaking career couldn't take off abroad. But in India, I started speaking regularly. My perspectives were so rebellious that I always ended up knocking down deeply-entrenched beliefs and impacting people for a massive change in their lives. This went on for four years across India.

One such assignment took me to Bangalore. It was a startup festival. The place was absolutely buzzing with energy with thousands of wannabe startup junkies receiving success-lessons from already-successful entrepreneurs. I heard someone talking about Marketing and Sales. It was the worst session I had ever attended in my entire life. I was supposed to address the same group later in the day on the idea of **Solopreneurship** (nobody else had ever spoken of it in India).

But after hearing the previous speaker, I couldn't resist changing my topic last minute. I spoke about how conventional marketing was dead and how Mr. Kotler made absolutely no sense. I spoke about the real decision-maker in the human body: the old brain/ the reptilian brain. I gave them an absolutely earth-shattering perspective about Positioning, Marketing, Sales, and Branding. The basis of this whole idea was rooted in brain-science. People were absolutely enamored. It related so much to them and their businesses that I had a record 700+ people staying up until the wee hours in the morning to speak to me. ***I had found my mojo***. I shifted to Bangalore and became a Corporate Storytelling Coach.

Prior to this, life had involved so much travel for me that I wanted a break from my travels. While talking to a startup client, the story of 'how-my-Harvard-dream-was-shattered' came up. And she was really intrigued. She was herself planning to write the GMAT and apply to top B-schools. I also told her about my prior experience in CAT, GMAT, and GRE training. She suggested opening a GMAT training center. She convinced me that I could impact many people in Bangalore by making their dream of an Ivy-League education come true. It sounded exciting. As I wanted a break from my travels, this seemed to be a good career option. Before I decided to take the plunge, I wrote the GMAT myself (on 23rd November 2007) and got a 770 score (this was without a minute of preparation). Later I applied to two of the programs at Harvard (MBA and Doctoral) and made it to both.

Life had come full circle. But my charm of a B-school had been completely lost.

I started training students for the GMAT and, in a matter of just three months, the popularity of my training reached stratospheric levels (I was the only GMAT trainer in India who had an official 99th percentile score report to showcase). I trained a record number of students with absolutely spectacular, gravity-defying results. I made 99th percentile (760-800 range) scores common lingo in India. So much so that when my students got a 750, they felt awful and wanted to retake the test.

*****

After having spent many years of my life as a successful Solopreneur, I luckily chanced upon the life- and career-changing book *A Whole New Mind: Why Right-Brainers Will Rule the Future* by Daniel H. Pink. After reading this book, I realized that I had wrongly prided myself for being a completely logical, linear, and mathematical person, and that I was fundamentally a right-brained person but had been working for many years in areas that accentuated the application of my left-brain. In this book Daniel Pink emphasizes the important of six right-brained attributes for big-ticket successes (design, story, empathy, symphony, meaning, and play).

Mathematics, logic, language, and reasoning, coupled with my information-base about the world, had made me successful thus far but this book made me realize that, by embracing these six attributes, I could expand my sphere of influence a thousand-fold. As suggested in the book, I attended various storytelling festivals in the world. I learnt the biggest lesson of my life: for big-ticket successes, my smarts had to be matched by my storytelling ability; nostalgia could no longer be my business model.

In a single day, this book made me go from 'data to design', from 'stats to stories', from 'segments to symphony', from 'math to meaning', from 'ego to empathy' and from 'proving to playing'.

Using the learnings from the Book, I launched a number of courses:

- **Life without a Boss** – the complete Solopreneurship course. The effect of this course was madness personified. Within months, hundreds of people quit their cushy (but lousy) jobs to live the life of their dreams.

- **Know the World in 24 Hours:** In 2011, during her ISB-interview, one of my brightest students, Rashmi, couldn't answer a simple question about the European Financial Crisis (read the full story in the chapter on Perspectives). This pained me a lot; I wanted to solve this epidemic called 'lack-of-reading-and-perspectives'.

And I launched *Know the World in 24 Hours*. My students at Harvard, Kellogg, MIT, Wharton, Booth, Columbia etc. absolutely vouched for this course. The impact was so massive that they started calling it the *compulsory 24-hour MBA before the* ***optional*** *24-month MBA*.

- **B.O.L.D.** Most women I met as my clients lacked one thing for sure: they were not BOLD and entrepreneurial. To this effect, I launched my course B.O.L.D. – Beware of Lady Dynamites – a complete blueprint for women Solopreneurs. The success of this program surpassed all my expectations. More about this program at the end of this chapter!

  The massive response to these programs can only be experienced in these video testimonials: https://www.youtube.com/watch?v=-hmR4qO0whY

- **N.E.U.R.O.-Seduction:** Whenever I guided my startup clients, I found them woefully lacking in the idea of Positioning, Marketing, Branding, Selling, and Personal Storytelling. To this effect, I launched the course N.E.U.R.O.-Seduction. **I believe it to be the most powerful idea for business, career, and personal life.** In no time, this program took my corporate trainings global. For this topic (as well as for Storytelling), I have been invited to speak in the US, the UK, France, Australia, Singapore, Malaysia, and of course India.

Are you Gorgeous or Ballistic?

Just 2 years ago, if someone had told me that I could earn $10,000 per hour, I would have laughed it off as a cruel joke on my capabilities.

But in September 2012, what I saw in London took my breath away. I saw some Professional Speakers making $1mn in a single day (by selling their Speaking Products from stage) and impacting thousands of lives.

Something just consumed me at that moment. I was completely enveloped by the new overpowering emotion; I had to be on such a stage. No matter what/how, this was the space I HAD TO be in. But to design a Speaking Product, I had to find a problem that I could justifiably solve. And the problem was lying there, in full glory. Whenever I met my clients, almost always I heard a sob-story about how they hated their bosses, how they wanted to break free, and how their jobs totally sucked.

They spoke about their passions but had no clue about how to convert their passions into profitable businesses. On the contrary, I believe that any passion can be converted into a flourishing business while helping the world in a big way. I had categorically identified a problem and a potential solution; even the book in your hands elaborates the same model: *From Passion to Profits*. You share your passion and I (and now this book) will tell you how to turn that passion into a profitable business.

So I gave myself a larger-than-life goal. For the first time in life, I announced to all my contacts that in June 2013 I would deliver a 2-day seminar called **Million Dollar Solopreneur (MDS)**. In a single day, more than 600 people registered. And I had a huge challenge in front of me:

- I had to find a way to mesmerize more than 600 people for two full days (18 hours of Power Speaking).
- I had to give people relevant content, tools, and strategies that would actually enable them to become dollar-millionaires.
- I had to give them a tangible step-by-step millionaire blueprint.
- I had to learn all the skills of Professional Speaking and apply each of them in real-time in front of so many people.
- I had to come across as an absolute authority on my subject but still come across as warm, approachable, funny, witty, 'in-the-moment', and extremely comfortable in my own skin.
- I had to learn all the delivery skills for large stages.

- I had to prepare all the content + collaterals (Power-Points, Handouts etc.)
- I had to market the event so well that 600+ people would actually attend it.
- I had to lace each of my sessions with numerous stories and a lot of humor.
- I had to keep them absolutely hooked, leaning on each word of mine for two full days.
- I had to present the talk so effectively that people would sell all my future offerings to themselves.
- I had to oversee all the operational aspects of organizing such a big event.
- I also wanted to collect on-the-spot high-emotion video feedback.

And I had nothing ready. Neither the skill, nor the content, nor the delivery, nor the stories, nor the jokes; for a rational person, this would have meant a perfect copybook example a career-suicide (of an already well-established career).

All I had with me was this irrational PASSION—this obsession, this insanity, this sheer lust, this absolutely overpowering emotion—that I had to master this skill and cut into the amazing world of Professional Speaking.

And, on June 15th and 16th 2013, I did manage to pull off the biggest extravaganza of my career with terrific élan and gusto. I conducted the event and was able to accomplish all the aforementioned points and more. Some moments of the event are captured here:

In less than 12 months, dozens of MDS-participants have created massive incomes and loads of free time. They love what they do, travel around the world, and are impacting this world in a big way. All these people have turned Professional Speakers/Authors/

Trainers/Consultants/Premium Coaches/Video Product Sellers in some uniquely claimed topics. These people are living in the dream-patch of their lives.

Here's some feedback collected LIVE (on the spot):

https://www.youtube.com/watch?v=p2WG2t6JmrY

Some of the snippets from the program can be seen here:

https://www.youtube.com/watch?v=KhrCOsM28SY

When the Unimaginable Happened

What happened in May 2013 (even before MDS in June 2013) was not even in the wildest of my dreams. After spending more than Rs. 50 lakh and after qualifying nine rounds of evaluations, I was invited to present my 90-minute talk at the Public Speakers' University, London and the Professional Speakers' Academy, London.

I presented in front of more than 1000 globally-renowned Professional Speakers, and my speech about my copyrighted model Tri-Summit Storytelling System (Sandeep's 25-Step Formula for Electrifying Storytelling) was evaluated as the best speech of the year. I was offered £10,000 (almost Rs. 10 lakh) for the 90-minute speech. As a result, I was invited to become the resident Ace-Mentor at The Professional Speakers Academy, London, the biggest Professional Speaking Circuit in the world.

Receiving the Ace Mentorship Certification at PSA, London

This membership opened the floodgates of opportunities around the world. I also created my video products that (today) continue to sell quite handsomely.

As a next step, I launched another ambitious offering: **Jet-Set Speaker** – *Be the Millionaire Messenger*.

The response to *Jet-Set Speaker* has been the best—breathtakingly incredible—among all my courses. People have gone on record (on camera) saying that they have not received any education even one-hundredth as great as this—ever in their lives.

Watch the following videos to experience it yourself:

https://www.youtube.com/watch?v=f_bmCYh_Stc

https://www.youtube.com/watch?v=9K81xJRwwf8

The Founder of Professional Speakers Academy, London liked my Jet-Set Speaker course so much that he purchased the entire model with all its seven components from me. Now this product is offered at both the Public Speakers University and the Professional Speakers Academy as part of their various courses.

Has your worldview ever been completely knocked out of alignment?

When I launched any of the aforementioned courses, I heard the same rant again and again from many of the prospective Solopreneurs:

> "My work life **sucks**! I don't love my job. I am just putting in hours and I don't bloody care so long as I get my paychecks in time. If I had a choice, I would run away today and do something that I LOVE doing. I have tried my hand at a hundred things. Anything I start, I don't do it for long. I give up on my passions again and again. I get inspired, and then I get lazy again. I **hate** workday mornings."

At least fifty people I know run training-programs on the lines of 'Follow Your Passion'. Most of what they say is stale, clichéd, misleading, or downright useless. To make matters worse, on most days, I find them lacking in passion for anything in their own lives.

How has something so crucial (passion) become one of the most misunderstood topics of the modern era?

I find the following lines completely clichéd:

- "Demand more from yourself than anyone else could ever expect."
- "Why live an ordinary life when you can live an extraordinary one?"
- "Let there be no difference between what you CAN do and what you WILL do."

Somehow these lines sound great but are never able to motivate people to take action. They don't have the power to move you because they fail to arouse any emotion. They address you at the level of logic. And passion knows no logic. It is one of the two strongest emotions (the other being fear). **Passion is completely irrational and instinctive.** That's why all the rah-rah passion theories make 'zilch' sense.

Now, this is what Tony Robbins says about Passion (he just nails it):

- "People are not lazy. They simply have impotent goals—that is, goals that do not inspire them."
- "Passion is the genesis of genius. If we can generate the right emotion inside of us, we can get ourselves to do anything."
- "Passion is something that consumes you, something that automatically makes you drop 99 things and focus on just one thing, something that makes you love your self-time, and something that makes you stop multitasking."

Do you notice the word *emotion*? Remember the root of all these words: Motion, Emotion, Motivation, and Motive—all have the same root meaning 'movement'. So if your so-called passion fails to move you (or others) to take action, it is actually not passion.

Confession time: By 2012, after having spent 16 years of my career as a Serial-Solopreneur, it would have been fair to assume (on my part) that I knew a thing or two about the word 'passion'. After all, I had read/watched almost every conceivable resource written/ spoken about passion. But ironically, at the age of 38, three things (rather, three tight slaps on my existence) changed my entire understanding of my deeply-entrenched *Passion Hypothesis*.

1. I happened to read the book *Talent Is Overrated* by Geoff Colvin. This book proved to be an absolute myth-blaster for my understanding of passion. I could relate to every word of this book, especially after conducting MDS. Chapter 11 of this book "*Where Does the Passion Come From*?" can change your life. It completely changed mine.

2. I read another book *So Good They Can't Ignore You: Why Skills Trump Passion in the Quest for Work You Love* by Cal Newport. This is the best-ever counter to the lame *'find-your-passion'* hypothesis. This book debunks all the myths about rah-rah passion theories and talks about passion in terms of skill-development/a larger-than-life goal. For the first time in my life, something written about passion resonated with me so deeply.

3. I also watched one of the rarest of rare video clips of Steve Jobs (wearing shorts) addressing his key stakeholders and advertising agencies. In this seven-minute video, Jobs explains what lies at the core of Apple. And the way he explained "Passion" and the entire Apple's historic 1997 campaign just BLEW ME AWAY. This single seven-minute clip changed something substantial about my life. https://www.youtube.com/watch?v=keCwRdbwNQY

For the first time, any advice on 'passion' made complete practical sense. The advice was: *Tie your passion to a challenge, a competence, a skill—a whole new level of mastery.*

Thanks to this one line, since 2012, my obsession for mastering absolutely insane challenges has seen a multiple-fold jump. Challenges such as the thrill of acquiring the supremely challenging skill of Professional Speaking have been fueling my passion. This strong, instinctive emotion called passion, in its truest form, is an insanely strong emotion. If channeled properly, passion can move mountains. It can make people kill (or go for the moon). After reading these three resources and seeing the direct, massive impact in my life, I came up with my own version of passion hypothesis: *The 5C's of Passion Drivers*: Competence, Challenge, Creative Expression, Congruence, and Contribution:

- **Competence** refers to developing new skills, learning new things. This is the biggest driver of passion.

  Your Competence Level Determines What You will Pay Attention to: When you don't feel competent, you tend not to pay attention to bigger challenges and opportunities—because you don't feel you can handle them.

  Your Competence Level Determines Your Choice of Tasks and Activities: When you feel capable and confident, you are willing to take on harder tasks. This generally leads to more learning and more success at work. If you feel incapable, you focus on the easier tasks and quickly become a slave to safety.

  Your Competence Level Determines Your Effort Level: Hard workers believe they can create positive outcomes with their effort, so they try harder. Expert performance studies have shown again and again that if you believe you are competent, you will work harder (and smarter).

  Your Competence Level Determines How Adaptable and Resilient You will be: This one has surprising implications for how stressful you will be in life and at work. If you trust your abilities and are more willing to adjust your course if something isn't working, you will get up faster when knocked down.

  Your Competence Level Determines Whether You will Lead or Follow: People who believe in themselves and their abilities take the reins at work and in life. They feel competent to handle challenges because they trust they will figure out the challenge as they pursue a new, grander vision. Sadly, if you don't trust your abilities, you can rarely see a grand vision for yourself or others, let alone actively, consistently, and courageously chase it.

- **Challenge** allows you to stretch your present capabilities.
- **Creative Expression** enables you to freely express yourself – your identity, your free-flowing thoughts, your rebellious ideas – these may include speaking, writing, drawing, painting, acting, dancing, singing, performing, cracking a deal, the works
- **Congruence** empowers you to be exactly the same outside as you are inside, where you can totally drop your guard, where you need no pretense or guardedness
- **Contribution:** If you really want to put a dent in the universe, your purpose must drive your passion.

So, if you really want your passion to operate at super-peak levels, give yourself a three to six-month long concrete goal that stretches you and makes you develop exactly one skill, and announce it to the world as a future offering: a session, a program, a video, a write-up, a story. Then for the next three to six months, you are sorted. Each moment will be spent passionately. By the end of these three to six months, hop on to mastering another challenging skill – and so on. Here are a few pointers about exactly how to pick a new skill, challenge, or goal:

- **Intrinsic Value:** Is this goal or activity something you are passionate about, would enjoy doing, and feel proud about? Would you do this regardless of extrinsic rewards like money, status, recognition, or power?
- **Autonomy:** Will you have decision-making authority in this pursuit? You need to feel as though you are in control and able to make things happen. No approval should be required for even one thing.
- **Future Identity:** Is this goal or activity relevant to your future identity, to how you see yourself, and to what you see yourself doing over the long-term in the future?

- **Utilitarian Value:** Is this goal or activity something that will lead to a useful outcome for you? Will you get something useful in life out of doing this?
- **Delay Time:** How long do you have to wait to get the benefits of trying and achieving? Is this goal or activity going to have quick and recognizable results that you can enjoy soon? Human beings are horrible when it comes to delayed gratification, and the longer we have to wait, the less our motivation to learn and try becomes.

A case in point is how I learnt the complete art and science of Professional Speaking:

The first thing I did was search the best Professional Speaking/ Public Speaking/Storytelling Coaches in the world. In a single day, I ordered 44 video/audio products (worth more than Rs. 34 lakh) from some of the best names in the business.

And thus started my 90-days of PURE LUST (yes, it was an obsessive involvement) – I spent close to 16 hours each day watching (or listening to) each of the programs, making notes, practicing, recording myself, reviewing my tapes, and finessing my skills. I spent more than 800 hours trying to master this skill. My madness reached such a level that even brushing my teeth, bathing, eating, or sleeping seemed like an absolute waste of time. Call it a dopamine- or an adrenaline rush, or what you will, but a full-blown orgasm wouldn't feel even one-tenth as orgasmic. I enjoyed the process so much that, 24*7, I visualized myself on that stage. The whole world had ceased to matter. I didn't speak to virtually anyone for months! I could kill to speak on that stage! I typed the following words in my phone and read each word aloud every morning, visualizing my upcoming live-stage performance as I read each word:

- Energized
- Superb
- Gorgeous
- Raring
- Smashing

- Unstoppable
- Fascinated
- Turbocharged
- Ecstatic
- Impassioned
- Fabulous
- Ballistic
- Tremendous
- Awesome
- Excellent
- Dynamite
- Magical
- Vibrant
- Exuberant
- Exhilarated
- Killer
- Incredible
- Phenomenal
- Jazzed
- Stoked
- Laser-like
- Enthralled
- Enraptured
- Passionate
- Compelled
- Driven
- Spectacular
- Extraordinary
- Monumental
- Invincible
- Soaring
- Explosive
- Brilliant
- Booming
- Insanely great

- Over the moon
- Doesn't get any better
- Cosmically charged

The products that I watched/listened to were:

Patricia Fripp (the best Professional Speaking Coach in the world)

1. Become a Speaking Star (along with five other speakers)
2. Compelling Stories
3. Help! I Have to Give a Speech
4. How to Build a Profitable Speaking and Consulting Business
5. How to Get, Keep and Deserve Your Customers
6. Meetings - Fun and Exciting
7. Preparing and Presenting Powerful Talks
8. Presentation Skills: Hollywood Style
9. Super Sales Presentations
10. Write It and They Will Pay
11. Create Your Keynote by Next Week (with Darren Lacroix)

Darren Lacroix

1. Connect
2. Healing, Hope, and Humor
3. Get More Laughs by Next Week
4. Say What
5. The Path to Powerful Presentations – How I Went from Chump to Champ
6. You Can Do This
7. Hope
8. YouTube It

Ed Tate

Energize, Educate, and Entertain

7 World Champions of Public Speaking Together

Connect With Any Audience

Craig Valentine

1. Edge of Their Seats Storytelling home study course
2. Create Your Killer Keynote
3. Dynamic Delivery Devices
4. Speak and Prosper
5. 7-Step Presentation Toolkit
6. Advanced Speaking Course
7. Better Selling Through Storytelling
8. Live from LA
9. Live from MIT
10. Starter Pack
11. World Class Product Creation
12. Own The Stage (with Darren Lacroix)

Andy Harrington

1. Elite Coaching Program
2. Winning Webinars
3. Marketing Mastery
4. Power To Achieve

Roger Love

1. The Perfect Voice
2. Vocal Power
3. The World's Greatest Speaker Training (with Brendon Burchard and Bo Eason)

Bo Eason

Personal Story Powerpack.

Toastmasters

1. 25 Years of World Champions of Public Speaking – International Speech Contest – Positions 1, 2, and 3 – overall 75 speeches
2. 20 Years of Humor – 20 Humorous Speeches
3. 20 Years of Keynote – 20 Keynote Speeches

Just to give you a secret, Patricia Fripp's products genuinely stood out as the very best.

To sum it up, if you truly want to fire your passion, give yourself a large goal and announce it to the world. Go out on a limb, develop a new skill, overcome a new challenge, and fire your PASSION all over again. The world can't wait to see you perform ... Passionately!

My life's current mission: I want to create more and more dollar-millionaires in this world using "The Solopreneur Blueprint".

In retrospect: If I hadn't read the book *A Whole New Mind,* none of these programs would have ever seen the light of the day. Thank you Daniel Pink!

TODAY

Every year, I spend an equivalent of eight months reading books, attending courses/events/webinars, meeting interesting people, traveling, and having scintillating conversations. LEARNING has never stopped. My life's philosophy can be summarized in just two words: **Student Always!**

As a Solopreneur, I have had the best roller-coaster joyride of my life. There hasn't been even a single dull moment in my life in the last 18 years.

To add to the thrill, every year I offer one completely unprecedented program that has never been offered by anyone else anywhere in the world; this philosophy has been the single most crucial driving force in my life so far. The journey has been outrageous fun—pure orgasm!

Phew! That's about My Personal Journey.

Back to you: What are you waiting for in your life?

*****

The purpose of your Personal Journey: Your personal journey must automatically position you as an expert in your 'claimed' topic. So this, in essence, is your **Expert Positioning Story**.

Example

Life Without a Boss: for most of my working life, I have lived a Solopreneur life (life without a boss). So my life story automatically positions me as an expert in this 'claimed' topic of mine.

Ask yourself this question: "Does my life-story automatically position me as an expert in my 'claimed' topic?"

Your story is crucial because there will always be some persistent questions that your clients (readers, listeners, or buyers of your products) will have in their minds before they actually buy any solution or a product from you. These may be:

- Why should I trust this expert?
- Why is this expert the right person for me to buy from?
- Why should I listen to this expert?
- Why should I read this expert's book?

In effect, they are looking for some of your credentials.

As an expert Solopreneur, the best credential you have is your personal positioning story – a story that automatically positions you as an expert in the topic that you have claimed. Nothing cements your place better in the eyes of the buyer than your triumph story (woe-to-win). Make sure that the story is relevant to your topic; if you are speaking about NeuroMarketing, the story of 'how I quit my job and am now following my passion' will be absolutely useless.

'No personal story' equals 'no trust', which, in turn, equals no sale. Imagine someone selling a workshop on better parenting without ever having been a parent. Who will buy a solution from this person? Imagine someone selling a stock-market investing DVD product without ever making money by investing in the stock-market. Or imagine someone offering "Entrepreneurship" training without ever having run a business. I am sure you get the point.

So, in the Solopreneurship space, your personal story is much more powerful than your degree or certifications. Also your best testimonial is a client's success-story (preferably a video testimonial), not your product's features/benefits. When your prospective client sees your client's success-story, she automatically tells herself a future-story: "if he could succeed by using this speaker's book/classes/training/seminars/video products, then using the same solutions, I will succeed too."

Let's read an example:

> "I was absolutely scared of speaking in public but, after attending Sandeep's "Jet-Set Speaker" program, I can speak to more than 500 people very effectively for hours together. In fact, I recently delivered a speech to a group of a hundred people and I got an absolutely raving feedback. I even made Rs. 7 lakh by speaking on stage. I highly recommend Sandeep's "Jet-Set Speaker" to everyone." The prospective customer will ask: "WHERE DO I SIGN?"

Once you have understood the importance of your story, the next obvious question in your mind will be: "How to craft my story?" But, before discussing how to craft your story, let's discuss the most effective definition of a story:

> "A story presents a pattern of cause and effect, while keeping the curiosity of the reader/listener intact."

The most crucial component of a story is **curiosity** (curiosity is nothing but a feeling of 'Why did this happen?'/'HOW did you manage that?'/'What happened next?'/'What did you do next?'—a sequence of cause and effect); the listener/reader must always have a sequence of "WHY"/"HOW"/"WHAT" questions throughout the story. If they have no questions, your story is over—at least for them.

How to Craft your Story – A Quick 10-point Checklist

1. **Curiosity**: Throughout your story, you must be able to arouse curiosity through *why/how/what* questions.
2. **Circumstance**: You must describe the situation/scene in such a way that the audience can visualize the scene as if it were happening in front of their own eyes.
3. **Characters**: Give description of at least a few characters in a story.
4. **Conversations in dialogues**: You must include dialogues in your story. It must not be a narration.
5. **Conflict**: A story must have a lot of conflict/struggle. The audience will be hooked to every word.
6. **Climax**: The conflict must reach a summit, a peak, a point of no return—a situation where it can't get worse than the 'present' moment.
7. **Cure**: Finally the conflict has to be resolved and life has to change for the better.
8. **Conclusion**: People like to know what happened as a result of the cure. So you must have a clear conclusion.
9. **Carry-out message**: A story must contain a message. If there is no message, don't tell your story in the first place.
10. **Callbacks**: Keep referring back to your story throughout your book, presentations, materials, speeches, blogs, websites, videos—everywhere.

CLIENT-TESTIMONIAL STORIES

Apart from your own personal positioning story, the success-story of your client (preferably on a video) will add to your already established personal credibility.

A useful format:

- Before
- Now
- Which means
- That is why

An example

BEFORE I worked with Sandeep, I had no clue that anything like Professional Speaking even existed; I just knew about Public Speaking. Also, I was extremely shy of the stage. Even the mention of speaking on stage used to give me jitters. I was just stuck in my job, hating each moment of it.

NOW, just after attending a three-day seminar 'Jet-Set Speaker' by Sandeep and applying his techniques, I have been able to establish myself as a Professional Speaker and I am making at least 20 times the money per month. In fact, recently I spoke to a group of 10,000 people*. I have a clear vision of where my business is going; I have a fully mapped out product tunnel and a clear strategy about how to attract more clients.

WHICH MEANS that I can now live the life of my dreams, spend more time with my family, and go on a holiday whenever I want. I don't have to exchange my hours for money.

THAT IS WHY, if you want to create a better life and an extremely profitable business as a Professional Speaker, I would strongly recommend you to attend Sandeep's program 'Jet-Set Speaker'. You will be able to live the life of your dreams. Your life will change, for sure.

My student, Karthikeyan, speaking to 10,000 people

PRODUCT STORIES

If you offer a unique product, you must tell the target audience the reasons for offering it in the form of a story. Here is an example of my 'product story' for B.O.L.D. – Beware of Lady Dynamites.

Product Story for B.O.L.D.

Some of the best days of my life were spent in the arms of another man's wife: my Mother!

If you were to see her career-graph, you would wonder: "Wow! This is what I want to live life like." All the glitz, glam, grandeur and the whole shebang were part of her daily life. But she was never happy. Not even for a day.

Her parents got her married her off when she didn't want to marry. I wonder why she succumbed but she did succumb. She wanted to go to the London School of Economics and Harvard Kennedy School of Government to study Public Policy and eventually work with The World Bank/The United Nations. I consider this an act of cruelty inflicted upon her by her parents. Most parents in India indulge in such cruelty at least once in their lifetimes. Why can't they leave their children alone after a certain age?

"Our parents don't prepare us to succeed; they prepare us not to fail."

Although she was more talented and much more capable than my father, she always played the second fiddle to him. She gave a lot of herself to make things work, sacrificed many of her foreign travels, and somehow could never excel as much as she wanted to. Beyond a point, she just kept on compromising even when a compromise was not required. It was as if she automatically assumed that the 'man' of the house had to be the undisputed leader of the pack. UGH!! I hated the fact that she depended on her husband emotionally to such an extent that she could never let her aspirations take wings. Except in one type of situation (when her children suffered), she never raised her voice within or outside of the household. She was successful, but she led an absolutely unfulfilled life.

She was not BOLD.

It didn't stop there: Among the dozens of relationships that I have had with super-successful women from all walks of life, I haven't met many truly liberated, bold, and independent women. It is no different with women from other parts of the world.

Before you read further, please understand one thing: I am not stereotyping; I am just sharing my experiences.

A lot of women feel 'stuck' in the life that (they feel) has been pre-ordained for them. Rarely do they break free, celebrate themselves, and live their bliss.

WHY DO YOU SEEK APPROVAL? Accept yourself completely the way you are.

Most of the times, this is what I hear:

- "I am sidelined from most of the strategic decisions in my company. If I try to put my point across strongly, I am labeled 'PUSHY'."
- "I want to pursue my passions of traveling, writing a book, painting, meeting people, and so much more, but don't really

seem to get anywhere. My life sucks and seems like a total waste."

- "I feel stuck—stuck in life, stuck in a career, stuck in the whole scheme of people around me."
- "I feel like running away from it all to a place where I don't hear all these voices on a daily basis (parents, partner, husband, boyfriend, relatives, society… blah blah blah!)."
- "I am stagnating in my career. I don't get the kind of growth or recognition that I deserve."
- "I hate expectations. Everyone expects me to do things in a certain way. Everyone expects me to fit in. I hate to fit in. I want to break away."
- "I am sick of endless explanations and justifications that I have to give people around me."
- "I want to yell at my boss and say, "YOU are an idiot", but would never dare to do so."
- "I don't/didn't want to get married, but I have to/had to get married. I don't/didn't have an option."
- "I don't trust people easily."
- "I trusted him blindly. I sacrificed my goals for him. And he doesn't seem to care a rat's a** about me."
- "I can't move on in my life. I can't get this guy out of my head."
- "I want to LIVE MY OWN LIFE completely on my own terms but it won't happen. People won't let me."
- "I feel I am living the life someone else designed for me."
- "I always try to help/please people but feel cheated every single time I do so."
- "Even if I try to make people happy around me, all I end up earning is a bad word for myself."
- "I want to be my own boss. But I freeze even before thinking of starting something on my own."
- "I am scared of speaking on big stages. I want to talk effectively on big stages but feel "Who will listen to me? What have I achieved?"

- "I want to come across as superbly-informed. I want to have intelligent and meaningful conversations with people around me. But I just end up gossiping and wasting time over drinks as I don't think I can really contribute meaningfully to an intelligent conversation."
- "I want to achieve superlative success, fierce independence, staggering recognition, and unparalleled happiness, but don't know HOW. I don't know how to change THINGS."

Also, as a reverse trend, a lot of women who are doing exceptionally well in their careers (earning 50 lakh plus salaries) tend to be emotional-wrecks when it comes to handling their personal/ professional lives and seem stuck in a life that they don't deserve/ desire.

What pains me is just one thing: why can't you give the maximum importance to your own self? Why does everyone else's opinion matter to you?

So long as you don't give the maximum importance to yourself, you will be absolutely unhappy. If you remain unhappy, nobody around you can ever be happy.

My Objective Behind this Course

I want to see every working woman in this country **entrepreneurial**: independent (financially and emotionally), liberated, and BOLD. Even if you are not an entrepreneur, you must be entrepreneurial in every walk of life.

Imagine a joyride that guarantees a transformation:

1. From USED-TO-BE to YET-TO-BE
2. From Lackluster to Blockbuster
3. From Mess to Magic
4. From Sulking to Scintillating
5. From Proving to Playing
6. From Job to Joy

7. From Free to Fee
8. From Vulnerable to Victorious
9. From HAVE-TO-DO to LOVE-TO-DO ... ***AND FINALLY***
10. From Passion to Profits ... *Solopreneurship*

Imagine what we (as a country) can achieve in just 2 decades if all women we come in contact with (right from the first influence on our lives: mothers, teachers etc.) become really BOLD and instill (in the coming generations) the wisdom of thinking BIG, the merit in taking RISKS, and the importance of being OUTLIERS. We will witness a happier, more entrepreneurial, more liberated, and BOLDER India.

Imagine if your mother had instilled in you: "I don't want you to join company X/Y/Z as an employee. I want you to follow your passion and create something sensational for this world: the next Google, the next Facebook, or the next Apple (or whatever your passion directs you to do). Just put a dent in the universe."

Beyond instilling this feeling, imagine if she had equipped you with the requisite tools to do so! WHOA! Can you even begin to imagine what difference this would have created in your life? This program provides all the tools for you to put A DENT IN THE UNIVERSE.

It is going to be the best joyride of your life. Are you boarding?

Craft your story now: I know what you are thinking: "All this is fine Sandeep, but I don't have a special story. I haven't achieved anything special. Why will people listen to me?"

My answer: You have an extraordinary story to tell this world but you have been conveniently ignoring it. Dig deeper; your story is screaming to come out.

Craft your story. This will be the single biggest investment in your career that you can ever make.

$$

PERSPECTIVES

I am not a troublemaker, dad.

For a very long time, my parents perceived me as a troublemaker. According to them, as a child, I always asked very embarrassing (or strange or uncomfortable) questions:

- At a zoo, when my father showed me the elephant and said: "Look, this is the most powerful animal on this planet." I asked him, "If it is so powerful, why does it live here in this jungle in such sweltering heat? Why doesn't it come to our place, drive us out, and sleep in the AC?"
- At a wedding I asked: "Why should the groom always be taller in a marriage? Why can't the girl be taller? Is there a law to this effect?"
- At a doctor's clinic, I asked the doctor: "Doctor Uncle, my parents always keep on asking me to study hard and be the topper of my school. What percentage did you get? Were you the topper, too?"
- Whenever I noticed a left-handed person, I would ask: "Why are so few people in the world left-handed? Why isn't the ratio 50:50?"

- At a superstore I asked: "Why is milk sold in rectangular containers (tetra-packs) whereas soft-drinks and beverages are sold in round (cylindrical) containers?"

For my parents, the list of such questions was endless. But somehow the only answer I got was: "Stop thinking about useless things. These won't be part of the exam. Focus on your studies."

Well, thankfully my mentor BD always encouraged me to ask all sorts of questions. In fact, he would get irritated if, during a discussion, I didn't ask some really penetrating and curious questions. According to him, curiosity didn't really kill the cat; it helped the cat find a new way, a better way. Curiosity is the lens through which **perspectives** emerge. Curiosity is the best thing to have happened to us (humans).

We could move from the jungles to the caves to the trees to arable land to villages to cities to Space—only because we always asked the question: "WHAT NEXT? What is our next frontier?" As humans, we have always challenged the status quo. Even in the modern context, if Galileo/Columbus hadn't challenged the status quo, we would have possibly still believed that the earth was the center of the universe or that the earth was flat or that there was only one way to reach India from Europe.

In fact, once BD showed me a painting by Paul Gauguin (created in 1897). Through his painting, Paul asked three quintessential questions:

- Who are we?
- Where have we come from?
- Where are we going?

You will find it impossible to believe it but I got a six-month long education as the answers to these three questions. The entire idea of the origin of the universe, the origin of species, evolution, brain-science, existentialism (philosophy), nihilism, technology, speculative intelligence, the fundamental nature of Man (humans), our place in the universe, speculations about death, afterlife, religion, spirituality—the list goes on. All this was laced with anecdotes, history, archaeology, paleontology, and research elaborating on some of the most seminal works of all times. Such is the power of asking the right questions.

Flying Car

Every day, you see garbage almost everywhere in India. Millions of people are so agnostic to the existence of this problem that piles of garbage all around them don't ever register in their minds. But one person sees this horrific situation, gets really pained by it, starts a garbage-disposal/waste-management company, and makes a huge difference. AND YES, makes millions in the process.

What is the difference between the people who conveniently chose to ignore the problem and the person who made millions? The difference is **PERSPECTIVES**!

Food for thought: *If you see a car and a bird together, do you think of 'flying car' and 'mechanical bird' immediately?*

Great business leaders don't know most answers that their teams do. They are great leaders because they can ask the right questions, challenge the status quo, and connect two things in ways that are beyond others people's perception. In fact, the biggest innovator of the modern era, Steve Jobs said, ***"Creativity is connecting the dots."***

What a simple, yet possibly the most powerful and profound definition of a concept that is otherwise considered vague, hazy, and fuzzy. What Steve meant here – if you see things in isolation, you can't succeed beyond a point. You have to synthesize, combine, connect, symphonize, make a big-picture, and have a holistic view, while thinking in a completely nonlinear fashion. In other words, you have to have an amazing ability to CONNECT THE DOTS between two seemingly disparate pieces of information and make some AHA! *meaning* that no one else previously had made. For a Solopreneur, this becomes even more important.

But the irony of today's workplaces is: they expect the employees to be creative but they rarely, if ever, give 'start-to-finish' ownership of that work. It is like telling a parent "You are supposed to be responsible only for the growth of arms in your child." When work is handled in isolated bits, it leads to just 'functional' rather than artistic, signature delivery. As a Solopreneur, you have no choice but to take care of your baby /your idea completely. So you have more chance to be creative.

If *curiosity* is one lens through which new perspectives emerge, *creativity* is the light that makes the perspectives truly visible, absolutely clear! More often, the problem is not with the answers we draft, but essentially, with the questions we present.

Imagine this question: 5 + 5 = ?

Can you be innovative with this answer? This is how our schools, colleges, and companies are. They focus on questions with just one answer. ZILCH CREATIVITY!

Now imagine the same question differently:

? + ? = 10

Suddenly the whole world of possibilities opens up. If you take positive numbers, negative numbers, zero, and fractions, there are infinite answers to this simple question. Simply put, this is INNOVATION.

As a Solopreneur, you have no option but to see things and make connections that others have failed to make. Let's see this in action:

Example 1

The mother of an adult daughter who has helped her daughter through puberty years comes up with a DVD/online video product: *How to help your daughter through those puberty years?* – An instant connection with millions of mothers of adolescent daughters worldwide who would love to get this product. If the product has real value and is reasonably priced, just a few hours of investment in this video can mean financial freedom for life for the creator, while she educates millions and impacts lives. This person may even be invited to speak to parents at school PTMs and many other places.

But this problem has been there. ALWAYS! So far, nobody has seen this as an opportunity. Only one person will see this problem as an opportunity, connect the dots, will have the right perspectives, and will make a difference ... **and make a fortune**.

Example 2

Climate Corporation: While driving to work for Google, David Friedberg observed that a bike rental company was closed on rainy days. Suddenly, an idea came to his mind: "How many businesses are affected by weather?" He founded a company that sells insurance to protect businesses from weather-related losses using advanced data analytics. The company examines weather data to provide insurance to farmers who can lock in profits even in the case of drought, excessive rains or other adverse weather conditions. In October 2013 Monsanto announced that it was acquiring the company for approximately $1.1 billion.

Again, so many people saw what David saw. And so many people know data analytics. But this man combined the two and created a billion dollars.

Example 3

Saveen Hegde and **Rohini Mundra** cofounded a Learning and Development company *"**7 intelligence**"*. Around the world, people crib about how pathetic and boring Corporate Trainings are. But these two took the problem head-on and founded the company with a simple mission: *"**Creating non-boring training programs!**"* In just 2 years of its existence, the company has gone global.

Well, obviously there are many companies offering non-boring training modules, but in their case it is not just an intrinsic quality but an outward claim. It is a mission and therefore simply bold.

Example 4

Freud versus Ramachandran: In April 2014, on a flight from Bangalore to London, I was seated next to senior executive from P&G. She happened to be reading the latest issue of Scientific American (***The New Century of the Brain***) and I happened to strike an awesome conversation with her about the human brain.

For almost nine full hours, we kept on talking about evolution, discoveries in brain science, NeuroMarketing, and a zillion other things about the most fascinating aspect of human existence: the brain.

She was completely taken aback by how I connected philosophy and mathematics (did you know that mathematics was a branch of philosophy earlier?), mind and brain, Sigmund Freud and VS Ramachandran, Reptilian brain and marketing, among many others. Her precise comment was: "I am not amazed by what you know about the brain. I am amazed that even when I know quite a lot, I never saw these things in connection; each piece was an isolated piece of information for me."

We exchanged our business cards, and the next morning I woke up with an email with the title: "Will you address the senior

Marketing team at P&G?" The following week, for a full day, I spoke to 60 senior executives.

Even McKinsey understands this:

The most coveted company at all the top B-School campuses around the world, McKinsey & Company, realizes the importance of 'connecting the dots' so well that, at the interview stage, it invariably asks some questions that test this skill.

A sample of such questions is given below. Check how many of these questions you can answer absolutely convincingly (so convincingly that McKinsey selects you); if as a Solopreneur, that is not what matters, regard this as brain gym!

Questions asked at McKinsey Interviews:

1. One country in the world (among about 200 countries) spends more than half the world's military expenditure. The trend has been so for the last 20 years. Even in peace times, why does one country (the US) spend so much on military? Give a complete analysis. You have to explain the answer clearly. You may go back to historical reasons if you think they are necessary.

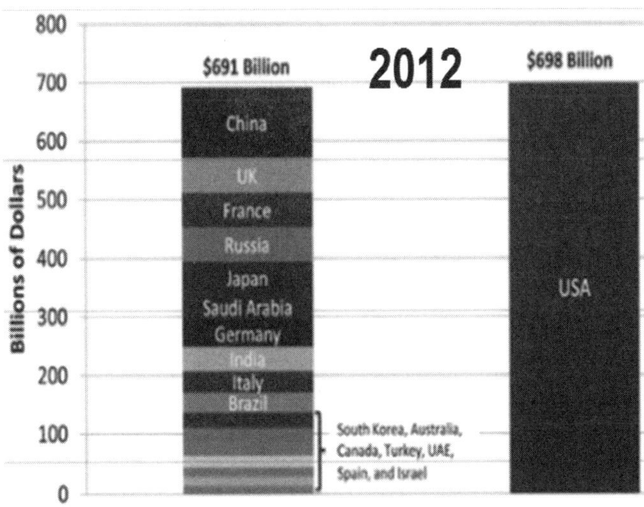

2. Why do we find it really difficult to express our feelings in words? We expect an extremely convincing answer with exact reasons. This question is extremely crucial to a marketer as marketing & branding is all about tapping into the feelings of people.

3. How can we combine Evolution, Brain Science, Storytelling, Marketing, Persuasion, and Sales to attain stellar results in all aspects of business and life? Explain completely by building a case with cogent arguments.

4. Rationally speaking, extreme sports, adventure sports, horror movies etc. shouldn't be popular (you could lose your life). Why are they still so popular? Give a complete analysis.

5. Estimate the number of car tires in the city of New York. Please understand that we are more interested in knowing your thought process than in the actual number.

6. Estimate the number of footballs in the city of New Delhi.

7. At Amazon meetings, one chair is always empty, but it never happens at Apple meetings. WHY?

8. If you have the liberty to remove one of the two persons from human history, whom will you remove – Hitler or Christ? And WHY?

9. Imagine that you have caught a 200 feet live, living, breathing, and walking dinosaur. What kind of money can you make with it within one year? Do the complete analysis.

10. If you were the CEO of Google, what would your personal mission be to make the company more successful in the short and long run?

11. Comment what the world would have been if the following had not existed (one by one):

    - Microsoft
    - The contraceptive pill

- The Bible
- The Printing Press

12. Comment on global-demographic trends and join as many dots as you can.
13. Comment on Variable Risk in doing business these days. What is it?
14. What could be the final frontier of technology (technological progress)? Explain completely by building a case with cogent arguments.
15. Comment on the word "Asymmetrical" by taking various perspectives that could directly apply to business- or life-success. Explain completely by building a case with cogent arguments.

Did you notice that none of these questions can be answered by knowing facts/having information alone? You need an understanding of the world as an intermeshed reality to be able to answer even one such question. And ultimately it's all a game of perspectives—perspectives on life, people, situations, everything.

As a Solopreneur (speaker/author), you will be appreciated more for novelty than for anything else. And the best novelty in the information-overloaded world is your **PERSPECTIVES**. I encourage you to develop this skill. Here is how you can start:

- **Have open-ended discussions with varied, interesting people.** I can't stress this enough. My biggest wish in life has always been to have an absolutely scintillating conversation with one new insanely awesome person each day. Don't waste time with people from whom you can't learn anything significant. After all, you become the combined average of the five people you hang around with the most. In the last 18 months, I have spent time with some of the best Solopreneurs/Professional Speakers/Authors in the world – both virtually and in person. If your peer-group is not helping you reach your goal, you must actively seek to change the group.

- **Travel not to relax but to learn:** The best way to accomplish this is to sign up for some really great events happening across the globe at least once every quarter. I have done so consistently for the last seven years and the results have been beyond words. When I am not traveling, I attend webinars from some of the best experts in the world at least twice a week.
- **Teach others:** When you learn something new, offer to teach that knowledge to others. Don't even think of money here. This is an investment in your life. When you teach, you learn, you grow, and you develop finesse in your field. I have been a teacher for over two decades, and I don't think anything else has helped me fine-tune my content more.
- **Write:** This is one of the most powerful ways to spark your creativity. A few years ago, I decided to write exactly 747 words every day. I wanted to fly all around the world delivering my talks and I thought of Boeing 747 as my mode of transport. I chose the number 747 as it would remind me of my mission daily. So, no matter what happens, I write something on most of the days. As a specific example, I wrote an article in October 2008 after the Lehman Brothers' collapse in the aftermath of the US Subprime crisis. The title was "Human Greed and Modern Capitalism – Does the Edifice Come Crashing Down?" This single piece of writing got me more than 1200 clients for my program *Know the World in 24 Hours* and got me speaking engagements in 16 different business-schools in India.
- **But most importantly, Read** at least one nonfiction book per week. No matter what happens, find time to read. This is one of the single biggest investments you can make in your career and life. Bill Gates was once asked: "How were you different as a child?" His answer: "One of the most important attributes that I had as a child was that I used to read a lot and still do." I can't emphasize the importance of reading enough. To me, reading has been equal to money, and more reading has been equal to more money. After all, the origin of all perspectives is

knowledge. If you wish to connect the dots, you must have some dots to start with. The more knowledge (dots) you have, the more connections you will make. Presenting three examples:

Example 1

I very strongly believe that if I had not read five life-impacting books before the age of 14, I would have been one of the millions of average, mediocre, and faceless commoners that dot almost every city of this country and would have obscured into oblivion long ago. Here are the five books:

BOOK 1 that changed me completely: This was a book about the Silicon Valley. I was absolutely enamored by the "maverick" culture and by the fact that wealth could be created on one's own terms with just one's brainpower. "You don't need capital or degrees to start any business" was the best education one could get in one's formative years.

Here is an excerpt from the book: "How do you go about building a tech city? One thing you've got to have is the proper 'tude (attitude). Silicon Valley's most valuable asset is its mind-set, a powerful merging of two behavioral strains: the macho, riverboat-gambler swagger of the original chipmakers who thought nothing of betting the company on a risky new idea, and the gently subversive high-tech idealism of early computer hackers. The resulting intellectual alloy counts you as a sellout if you don't try to make yourself a billionaire. This attitude is where a lot of Valley wannabes, particularly those outside the United States, fall short. But it's hard to overcome centuries of tradition that honor the very qualities that Silicon Valley loathes: aversion to risk, lifelong fealty to an employer, willingness to work within a strict hierarchy." This has been one of the most impactful ideologies to have guided my existence so far.

My lifelong learnings from this book:

- Courage and Risk-taking are quintessential to big successes. Dare to dream, take that plunge. Risk all you have!

- Follow your heart: No matter what happens, never do what you don't love. FIND what you are truly, insanely, and madly in love with and you won't have to "work", ever.
- Swim upstream. Breed and feed iconoclasm – the single most crucial attribute that separates us from the rest of the faceless commoners in the world.

BOOK 2 – the book that has had the maximum impact on me in my entire life and career: I was gifted the book *Fountainhead* when I was 12. This has been the most powerful book I have ever read. I have read it more than a dozen times. All the other books by Ayn Rand (*Anthem, The Night of January 16th, We the Living, Atlas Shrugged*) and her Objectivist philosophy were etched in my mind, soul, heart, and overall persona. It took me a while to understand all of it, but the impact that it had on me was unbelievable.

My lifelong learnings from this book (and Ayn Rand's other works):

- Have very strong convictions (obviously extremely unconventional) about what you do. Never compromise your belief/value system.
- One can live life absolutely on one's own terms. One person can take on the whole world.
- Excellence (being the "best in the world" at what one does). You must belong to the top 1% talent in the world at whatever you choose to do. Or else, your existence is absolutely 'third-rate'.
- Money will follow you if you follow your love, convictions, excellence, integrity, and courage.
- Free-market capitalism is absolutely necessary to unleash the Solopreneur in you. The animal spirits needed to create something insanely great could never flourish in socialism.

BOOK 3 that changed me: *Cosmos* and *The Dragons of Eden* by Dr. Carl Sagan: Brilliant books! These books awe, entertain, educate, and transform. All the perspectives about Natural Sciences, Physical Sciences, and Biological Sciences will become clear to you. There have been so many learnings from these two books that I can give sessions all my life and keep making money. The wealth of knowledge, mature perspectives, multi-disciplinary approach and the idea about the Universe we live in will be engraved in your brain forever. The Triune model of the human brain (discussed in *The Dragons of Eden*) is the single most powerful concept that I have known in life.

Meanwhile I developed interest in other disciplines as well: I have been an avid reader of History, Economics, Psychology, and Philosophy – apart from the already developed interests such as Astronomy and Evolution (courtesy Dr. Carl Sagan).

History: I read some books about world history and developed a strong interest in the subject. I feel one must read history. Today I can comfortably talk about the history of almost any place in the world. The lessons drawn are much more important than knowing the facts. Imagine this: if you find the reasons for the missing entrepreneurship in Indians but inherently present in the Europeans and Americans are deeply entrenched in history, you may be completely enamored.

Economics: What to say about this discipline! Economics is central to our existence. I have had an extraordinary interest in this subject: Free-market capitalism, markets, money-markets, Stock-markets, Capital Markets, Laissez-faire, Macro-economic Policy etc. all have fascinated me always. Capitalism's infallible promise and communism's failure to deliver have steered the course of my business life so far. For the last 20 years, I have not missed even one issue of *The Economist*.

Psychology: I am inherently interested in psychology. Your understanding of the 'human mind' gives you an extraordinary edge in business. For example, I attribute more than 90% of the success of Apple to its extraordinary understanding of 'how to rule the mind of the customer'. According to me, there is not even one discipline in practical life that can detach itself from psychology. Everything about Marketing, Branding, Advertising, Media, and PR thrives on capitalizing on the vulnerable human psyche. Even the most mathematical/ technical disciplines in the world (hard-core finance, software, cell-phones, laptops, for example) don't thrive at all if they don't understand how to rule the mind of the consumer. Psychology is everywhere. You just need to keep your eyes and ears open.

Philosophy: To me philosophy is not an abstract, boring idea. Philosophy is a 'living' thing. It is what you fundamentally believe in. I have read the entire works (more than 35 books) of one of the most influential philosophers of the twentieth century – Bertrand Russell, believed to be the biggest polymath of the twentieth century. Russell's work touches upon all disciplines of life. Philosophy is not a separate science. Philosophy is life. Philosophy is wisdom. Philosophy is about perspectives. Without a guiding philosophy, life has no meaning. Think of this in business: every company worth its salt puts its vision, mission, purpose, and core values – the guiding philosophy - at the forefront. But possibly no company puts its 'strategy' on the plaque. This is not a PR gimmick to have a philosophy for your own life. Without it, we are more like animals.

BOOK 4: the best business book I have ever read: ***Positioning*** by Al Ries and Jack Trout. I have imbibed this book in everything I have done in each of my life's interactions with anybody. There has not been even a single day in my life when I have not lived *Positioning*.

My lifelong learnings from this book:

- The battleground in business is the mind of the customer. If you can live there, there is no marketing, selling, or branding required.
- Anything can be sold with conviction and the right positioning. What more proof do you want than Coca Cola having been the number 1 brand in the world for 70

consecutive years (from 1935 to 2005) despite being one of the most useless products (containing only water, sugar, CO_2, and color). This is the magic of Positioning.

- Positioning can create customer evangelists, not just loyal customers.

BOOK 5: Alvin Toffler's Trilogy (*Future Shock, Third Wave,* and *Power Shift*) was one of the most impactful series of books that I have ever read. This series opened my mind to the idea of things to come (not the science fiction way, though). Imagine someone predicting the impact of the Internet in 1970 the way it is actually felt today. He predicted the "Digital Revolution" when nothing of that kind existed. Absolutely Brilliant!

My lifelong learnings from this series:

- One needs to learn, unlearn, and relearn very fast in today's era. Adaptation is the name of the game.
- Technology will define the businesses of tomorrow.
- Leaders who can anticipate and foresee the shape of things to come can surely win in the marketplace.

Example 2

I want to share a story about one of my students who hadn't been a reader; sadly, she had to pay a huge price for this lack at a really critical juncture of her life.

Rashmi trained with me for the GMAT in June 2010. Before she joined, I happened to counsel her. I asked her a few usual questions: "What are your career goals? Where do you want to do your MBA from? What are your passions?" She said: "I want to just earn a lot of money and I want to travel – especially I want to go on a long vacation to Europe. I am in love with the place. Although I have never been there, Europe has been nothing short of an obsession for me. But as of now I don't have enough money to afford such a vacation."

Coincidentally, in 2011, Europe was facing the worst economic and financial crisis of modern times. The European Financial Crisis was undoubtedly the biggest news story in Global Finance between 2010 and 2012.

She was an engineer working with an IT company. She scored really well on her GMAT and applied to many schools. But she had no fixed career goal. She took some help from an external admissions-consultant and he advised her to mention Finance as the specialization in her MBA (although she didn't know anything about Finance). The first school to send her an interview-call was ISB.

She was extremely nervous before her interview (in January 2011). She reached the venue much earlier (the interview was at 1 PM and she reached before 11 AM), and since a particular slot was free, the coordinators asked her if she would want to wrap up earlier. In the nervousness she said 'YES'. She entered the room and sat in front of two elderly looking gentlemen. After the pleasantries were exchanged, the first interviewer started reading her CV and her essays. She sat there, feeling really nervous.

Interviewer 1: "Rashmi, you have written that you want to specialize in Finance."

Rashmi (*I am gone today*): "Yes sir."

Interviewer 1: So can you tell us about the biggest news story in Global Finance as on date?"

Rashmi: "I beg your pardon."

Interviewer 1 (a bit irritated): "Can you tell us about the biggest news story in Global Finance as on date?"

Rashmi: ... ...

Interviewer 2 (exasperated): "Can you tell us something about Europe?"

The moment she heard this word (EUROPE), her eyes lit up, her nervousness was gone, and she started smiling.

Rashmi (smiling): "Europe is one place that I have always wanted to go to. I have been totally smitten by it. If had enough money, I would leave everything and go on a vacation there. But as of now I don't have that kind of money with me. Europe is etched in my memory. I have grown up watching Europe on television and in films. Right from Switzerland's tulip gardens, to The Swiss Bank, to Swiss watches, to France, to Paris, to French fashion, to French wines, to French taste, to Britain, to the cosmopolitan nature of London, to Wimbledon, to Harrods, to Lords ..."

Interviewer 2 (completely irritated): "BUT!!!, this is not what I was ...

Rashmi (smilingly continues): "... to Spain and la-*tomatina*, to Italy and Gondola rides, to Greece and serene beaches ..."

Interviewer 1 (almost pulling his hair apart): "Rashmi, what about the financial crisis?"

Rashmi (confused): "I just told you that I have some financial crisis as of now. That's why I can't visit Europe."

And so on and so forth ... the interview proceeded.

Just after the interview was over, Rashmi called me and screamed: "Sandeep, I am sure I am making it. For the first one minute, it was bad. Then they asked me about my favorite topic: Europe. And in the next 29 minutes, I KILLLLLEEEEDDD it."

I asked: "Exactly what were you asked?"

Rashmi told me the whole story. **And my heart sank!**

All I could ask was: "Rashmi, where else have you applied?

She obviously didn't get through. When she connected with one of the interviewers on LinkedIn, she asked why she didn't make it. And the interviewer sent her a mail that said:

"Be a reader to be a leader."

As I have shared earlier, I got so pained by this experience that I started the course *Know the World in 24 Hours*.

Example 3

When I talk about innovation and Design Thinking, I talk about a model called, *The Design O.C.E.A.N.* Here OCEAN stands for:

- Observing
- Connecting the dots
- Experimenting
- Asking questions
- Networking

The model is inspired by the book *The Innovator's DNA* by Clayton M. Christensen (and others). The book says that there are just five main traits that separate best innovators from the rest of the people. The traits are: Questioning (Asking questions), Observing, Networking, Experimenting, and the most important of it all, Associational Thinking (Connecting the dots). I am offered Rs. 1 lakh per hour to speak on Innovation and Design Thinking. Do you still doubt that Reading = Money?

"Questions Are The Answers" said Allan Pease in his book by the same title. I couldn't agree more. So, be curious, meet interesting people, have interesting conversations, read, write, and travel ... but never stop asking questions. You will have insanely great perspectives.

I'd like to end this chapter by sharing with you one of the most inspirational stories of my career. My student from MIT-Sloan sent me a mail that will tell you the importance of perspectives. I am mentioning only the relevant excerpt.

> After I made it to MIT-Sloan, I visited Sandeep once as I had a very embarrassing confession to make. I hadn't read a single book throughout my life and I was going to a business-school that was ranked among the top-5 business-schools in the world. I felt quite bad about this and somehow believed that I wouldn't ever be able to contribute to the discussions at the school. I was terribly scared... "What will I do at MIT? Will be a misfit? How will people

react to me?" When I expressed this concern to Sandeep, he suggested to me something that totally changed me and WILL change this world soon.

Would you believe this? Sandeep asked me to author a book; YES, you heard it right. He asked a person who had never read a single book all his life to write a book.

As part of the conventional icebreaker, I was supposed to introduce myself at MIT (to batch-mates, seniors, faculty, and the Dean). This is the pitch that Sandeep suggested:

***

"I come from a country where the habit of reading is never encouraged. I grew up without reading a single book all my life (apart from the requisite textbooks). When I got my final admit, I felt that I would be completely out-of-sorts with the kind of crowd I was going to face at MIT. I really wanted to fix this. BUT there was a problem. Like most people in my country, I am an extremely slow reader and it may take me a lifetime to read and understand even a hundred books. So I have a different solution. I want to solve this problem of "non-reading" for myself and for the entire world by doing the following:

I want to come up with just one book that has only 250 pages, each page having the wisdom of one of the 250-must-read, life-changing books and want to make this one book compulsory reading for all the school children in the world. Before they leave school (let's say between 16 and 18 years of age), they will have to clear an exam based on this book's content. Imagine if we can help all the children in the world to get the life-impacting wisdom of the 250 best titles in the world, what this world could be in the next 10-15 years!

I know this is an audacious project, which a nonreader like me can never dream of accomplishing alone. I want to use the collective intelligence of this MIT-class (we are among the sharpest people in the world) and publish this book through MIT Press.

Picture this: If I were to come to YOU (people in the audience at MIT) tomorrow and ask you the name of that one book that has impacted you so much that you would want every person in the world to read before they die, and if I ask you to give me 15 minutes of your time to tell me the precise personal lessons that you have drawn from that one book, will you give me 15 minutes of your time for this world-changing idea? I will video-record each interview, give you credits for your contribution, and share the video of your exact conversation on YouTube. One page in the book will belong to YOU. Each one of YOU will have authored this book. Moreover, I want MIT to publish this book from the MIT Press and release it on an international platform. I am not doing it for money. I am doing it to change the world. With its reputation and clout, MIT can be instrumental in making it mandatory curriculum in all the schools around the world. Imagine the changed world in just 10 years because of your efforts ... because of OUR collective efforts. This is the best crowd-sourcing project you will ever be a part of.

Will you give me 15 minutes of your time to change the world? I can't do this alone. I need your help to change something about this world. I am on a world-changing mission. Are you boarding?"

***

What's more: the first interview I did was that of the Dean of MIT-Sloan. Almost every day, I am collecting the stories of personal transformation from my batch mates, alums, faculty members, and many more people at the campus; I am working insanely on this book.

The biggest outcome of this pitch: every student at MIT wants to meet me and contribute to this cause. They are chasing me and want to make friends with me. I would have been an obscurity but this pitch made me a true celebrity. Someone who was scared to go to MIT is a celebrity at the same place today. Imagine how well this will serve me for a lifetime. I will have a loyal network of 1000 future CEOs with me all the time. I am sure without this idea, I would not have made even 10 friends; today, more than 1000 people on campus want to be my friends. WHOA!

Just because I could connect the dots (connecting 'the lack of reading skills' to 'writing a world-changing book'), I could get such a testimonial.

So invest in building absolutely novel and unique perspectives. You can multiply your current level of success by a factor of 10 (or even 100) with novel perspectives.

$$$

PRODUCT

YOUR UBS – UNIQUE BRANDED SOLUTION

Inspired by a pimp!

In May 2013, when I presented my Tri-Summit Storytelling System at the Public Speakers University/Professional Speakers Academy in London, people liked my speech and my storytelling model so much that during each break I was surrounded by a huge number of people who asked me just one question: "Where can I buy your products?" This really hit me hard. I personally was not taking my own potential seriously. Absolutely everyone was selling their products. Someone jokingly told me that even a pimp had recently written a book and was designing his video products!

If I had had a (video) product, I would have made more than 200 sales that day. ***Lesson learnt the hard way!!!***

After coming back to India, I acted really fast. I started selling three of my offerings as video products. As of now, I offer video products to almost all of my 'live' programs.

In your journey as the Million-Dollar Solopreneur, one of the major ingredients is A PRODUCT, a solid offering. That solid offering is what I call your own **Unique Branded Solution (UBS)**. And, I am not talking about the medium here. A book, a DVD, a video solution, or a workshop is not your product; these are just mediums for your product to reach out to your audience. What I mean by 'your product (your UBS)' is a framework, a model, or a structure around your product so that people can "see" it, "feel" it, "get" it.

Imagine this: In a book, you may loosely talk for 400 pages about how to be an effective manager/leader, and there will be hardly any takers. Or you may create the first-of-its-kind billion-dollar speaking-and-training-enterprise by writing the best selling management book (absolutely commonsensical wisdom packaged beautifully) of the last century:

The Seven Habits of Highly Effective People
(Dr. Stephen Covey)

You and I both know that the wisdom offered in this book is nothing new. If asked how to be effective, even without reading the book, a large number of people on this planet can talk about almost the same stuff as Dr. Covey does in this book. So this begs the question: what made this book the one of the bestselling Personal Management books of all time?

The answer: a model, a structure, a UBS.

Let's see the model in some detail:

- It contains a **visual**: a visual model is extremely easy for people to "get". You may think of anything from a circle, a pyramid, a square, a flower, a tree... whatever. But a visual model is immensely useful. It is a great **'tangibility'** tool. This particular model talks about various stages. The first stage is to move from Dependence to Independence (this can be done in three ways: 'Begin with the End in Mind', 'Be Proactive', and 'First Things First' – these three contribute to your Private Victory). The second stage is to move from Independence to Interdependence (this also can be done in three ways: First Understand, then be Understood; Synergize, and Think Win-Win – these three contribute to your Public Victory). And finally, at each stage of

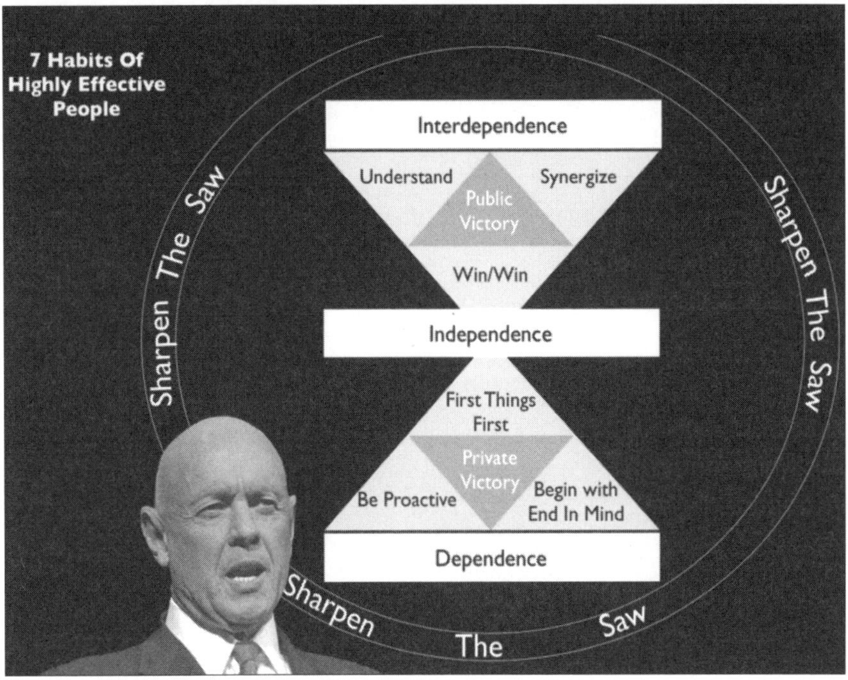

Dr. Stephen Covey's Model on *The Seven Habits of Highly Effective People*

the game you need to keep on Sharpening the Saw (shown in the outer circle), which means, whether you are at the first or at the last stage of the model, you need to keep on learning new things.

- It contains a STEP-BY-STEP **numbered** model: seven habits. We understand really well in steps; steps make the whole process very 'tangible', very doable. Otherwise rambling through 400 pages without having a sense of a model can be very frustrating to a reader.
- For 25 years, Dr. Covey taught the same model to millions of people in various workshops around the world; now his son is expanding his billion-dollar enterprise. This is the power of packaging the same age-old wisdom in a tangible model.

Let's see a few more models:

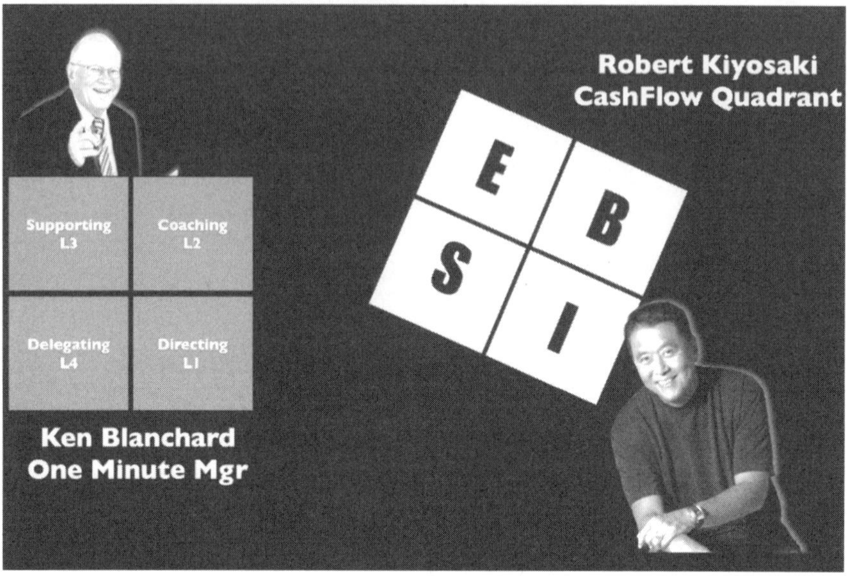

Two of the most famous books of the recent times, *The One Minute Manager* by Ken Blanchard & *Cash Flow Quadrant* by Robert Kiyosaki, follow a simple **visual** (quadrant) model. Both these authors own multi-million dollar speaking/training/consulting businesses.

The funny bit is that every manager already knows what Ken Blanchard is talking about. Directing, Coaching, Supporting, and Delegating are the obvious functions of an effective manager. But because of a model, the book sold millions of copies.

Robert Kiyosaki went one step further: he didn't even give the names of the steps in his quadrant; he gave just the initials. And Kiyosaki is one of the most sought-after global speakers. A model definitely helps.

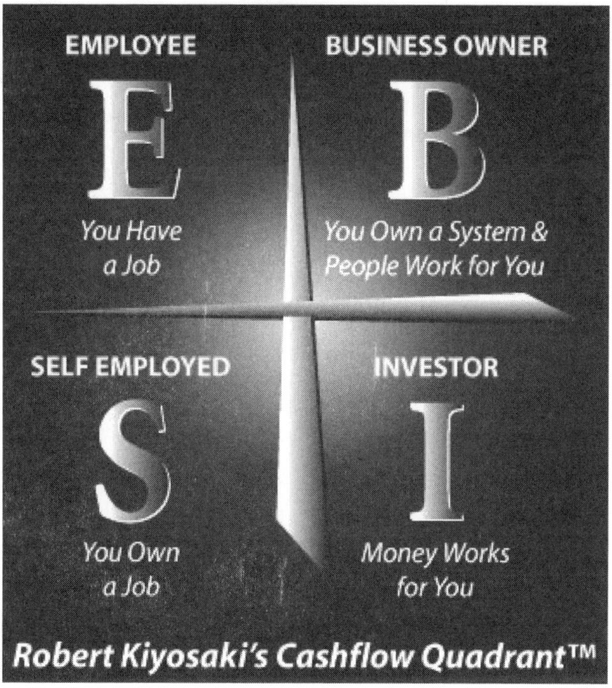

Let's see two more examples: **Maslow's Hierarchy of Needs** has lasted strong for 70 long years not so much because of the contents of his theory but because of the pyramidal structure that Maslow assigned to his theory (a **visual** model).

And lo and behold: Tony Robbins, the most shining example of Solopreneurship of the modern era, simply adapted the entire Maslow's model, renamed the steps, added one new step (uncertainty), and created his visual/numbered model of **Six Human Needs**.

And as a Solopreneur, Tony Robbins has made the maximum money from stage in the whole world, EVER! Picasso had a saying: "Good artists copy; great artists steal." Seemingly, Tony took Picasso's advice just too seriously.

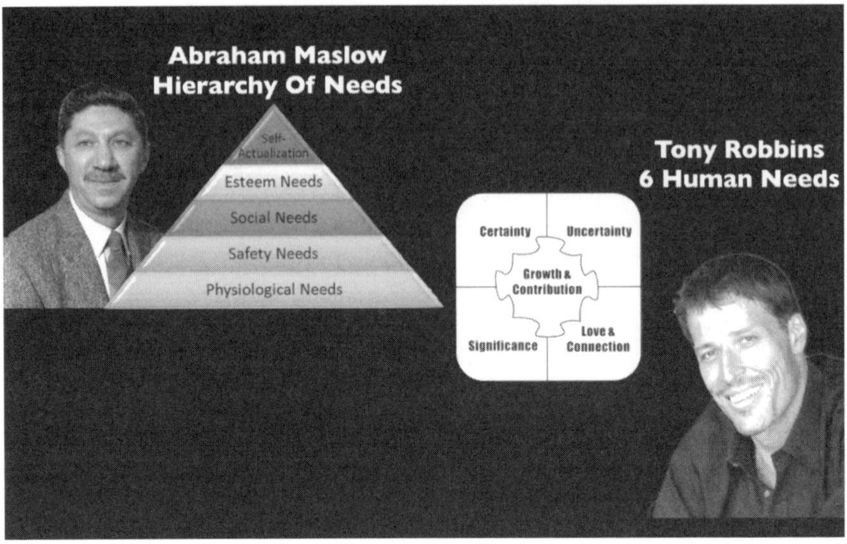

The moral of the story: the most obvious and commonplace wisdom, if packaged, modeled, and presented correctly, can make you millions.

We have seen two models so far: a **visual** model and a **numbered** model. Let's examine one more model: The **ACRONYM** model. Among the countless other books/products that follow this model, one of the most successful books of the modern times, *Made to Stick* by Chip Heath and Dan Heath, clearly stands out with its SUCCESs model. (see next page)

One of the most effective models is an **ALLITERATION** model. Some of the best Solopreneurs/teachers around the world use this amazing model to great effect.

- Craig Valentine (in his keynotes) uses 3G's to Greatness and 4R's to Remarkable Results. He owns a multi-million-dollar speaking business.

MADE to STICK
SUCCESs Model
SIMPLE
UNEXPECTED
CONCRETE
CREDIBLE
EMOTIONAL
STORIES
www.MADEtoSTICK.com
Why Some Ideas Survive and Others Die
MADE to STICK
Chip Heath & Dan Heath

- Philip Kotler's original 3C's and 4P's of Marketing.

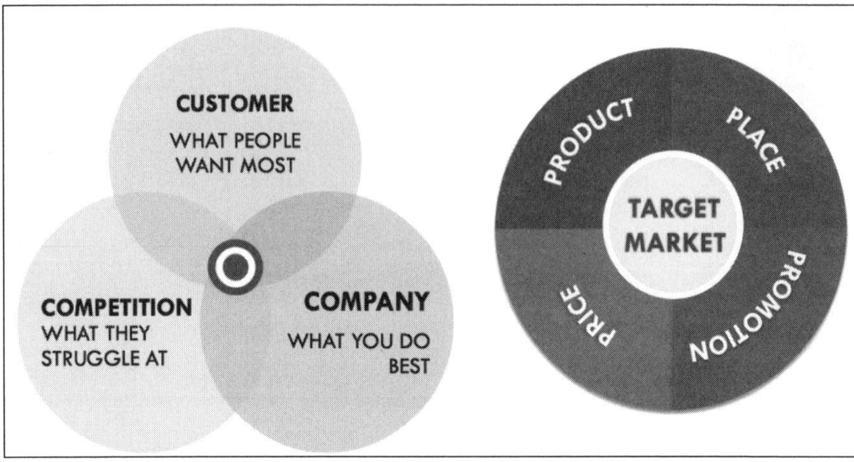

Throughout my life, I have also used these four models (visual, acronym, alliteration, and numbered) to create my UBS's.

Let's see a few:

The Solopreneur Blueprint – from Passion to Profits (alliteration + visual)

This whole book has been written around this model. The model tries to show you how you can become a Million-Dollar Solopreneur by following the exact steps mentioned here.

The Jet-Set Speaker System (the background here is an airplane – a visual model). Within the same model, there are a few ACRONYM models such as The Stress Free Speaker S.Y.S.T.E.M., S.T.A.Y. and Pay Positioning, and Kick-S.T.A.R.T. Content Creator.

The truncated **Tri-Summit Storytelling Model** (Alliteration + Visual):

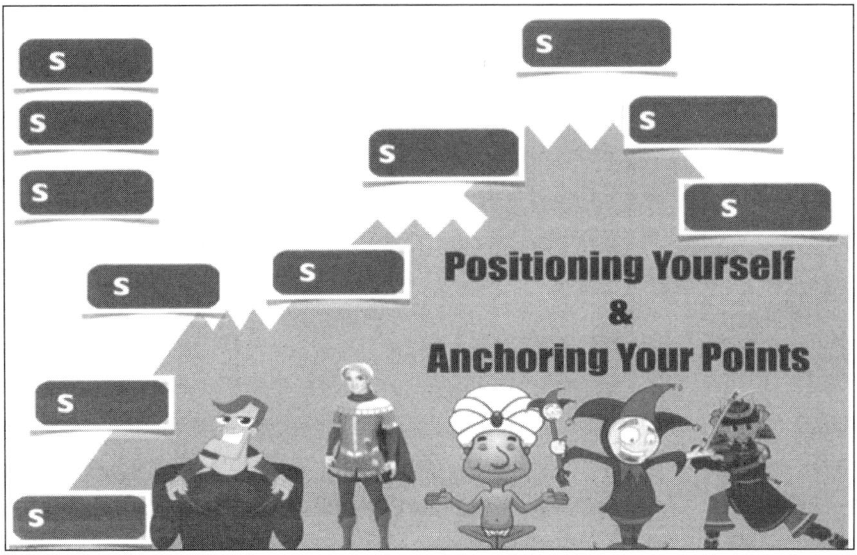

Each letter S in the above model stands for a specific attribute of a well-told story.

The **Engagement Matrix** for engaging your audience (Visual + Alliteration):

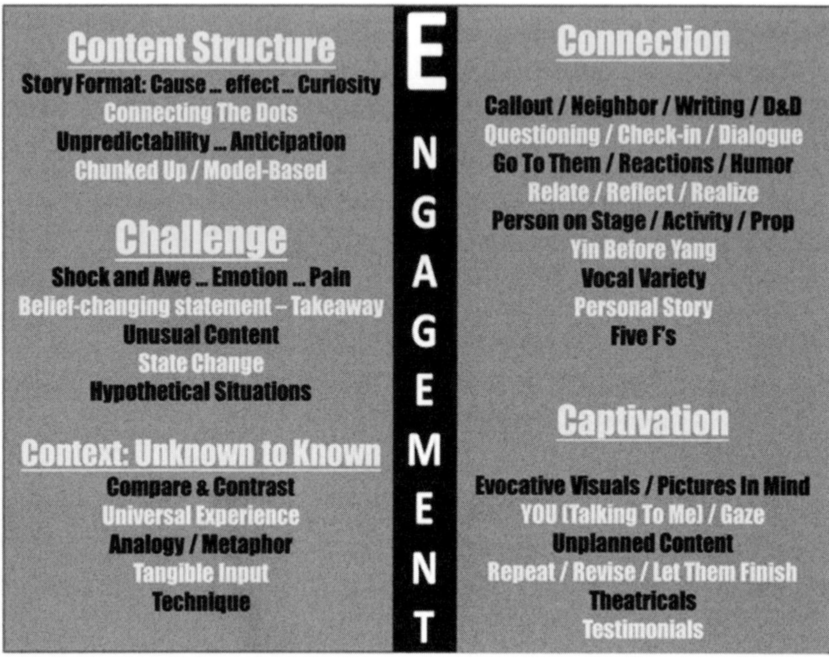

Another Visual + Numbered model that I have used very successfully is called the **Rapid Results** Generator:

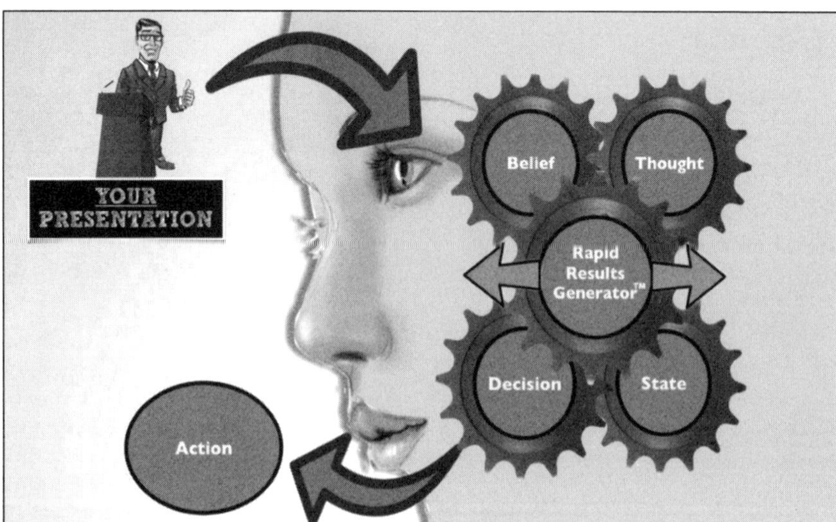

I am personally a huge fan of Acronyms. Some of the acronyms that I have used very successfully are:

- The Design O.C.E.A.N. (Observing, Connecting the dots, Experimenting, Asking questions, Networking)
- A.P.P.E.A.L. – Adorable Personal Positioning Exuded All Life
- B.O.L.D. – Beware Of Lady Dynamites
- The I.M.P.A.C.T. Work Equation (Inspiration, Mastery, People, Alarm, Contrast, Thrill)
- N.E.U.R.O. Seduction (Novelty, Emotion, U-focused, Rebellion, Objectivity)
- O.C.T.A.V.E. formula for acing GMAT Reading Comprehension (Opinion, Contrast, Tone, Avoid, Verify, Eliminate). **This acronym has given me millions extra in business.** When I didn't have a video product, students overseas came to study this model in my classroom sessions.
- Kick S.T.A.R.T. Content Creator – Salting, Teaching, Anchoring, Relating, Takeaway/Technique
- Stress-Free Speaker S.Y.S.T.E.M. – State, Yourself, Stance, Tonality, Eye-Contact, Movement
- S.T.A.Y.-and-Pay Positioning – Subject, Time, Audience, Yourself
- From S.T.U.C.K. to S.T.A.R. – from "Sore Truths Under Corporate Truths" to "She Turns A Rock-star"

Also, the *"Seven Steps to a Top-One-Percent Business"* is a step-by-step (**numbered**) model that I use very often.

Think about your solution. What models can you create around your model?

GUIDELINES FOR CREATING YOUR UBS

- **Less is more:** Don't reveal your full solution to your audience. Your UBS is supposed to be a map, not the territory it represents.
- **Keep things simple:** It is important to make sure that your UBS doesn't complicate things. It should reveal just a little while arousing immense curiosity. So, essentially, in the UBS, you need to sell your **Exper-TEASE** rather than your **expertise**.

Adapt Existing Models

There is no harm in adapting a model so long as you can add your signature to it. For example, almost all the storytelling models that I have seen follow Joseph Campbell's "The Hero's Journey" model; still, each model is unique in its own way. To get to that level, you need to know what all is available in the world. You must do the following to fuel your creativity (essentially, you need to experience it all):

- Read books from different genres
- Take trips to new destinations
- Meet people in fields different from your own
- Attend various Conferences/Webinars happening across the world

The more you experience how other experts are doing things across the world, the more your mind opens up to new possibilities. As an example of how you can create your UBS from scratch, I am mentioning how I came up with the model for the "Jet-Set Speaker" program. The following five steps will help you immensely:

1. Research/Review

As already shared, I spent close to 800 hours studying all the products offered by Patricia Fripp, Darren Lacroix, Ed Tate, Mark Brown, Craig Valentine, Andy Harrington, Roger Love, Brendon Burchard, and Bo Eason. You must do the same in your niche:

1. Find the top 5 experts in your niche.
2. Buy their products (books/CDs/DVDs/manuals/white papers/reports etc.)
3. Note all their points of wisdom.
4. Write down all the truths agreeable to you.
5. Consider the models they have used.
    - How have they chunked their information?
    - What is superfluous and can be dropped?
    - What needs to be added to make it better?

2. *Reverse Engineer*

For me, it was helpful to think about the very best speech of my career (at Google).

1. Visualize your past peak performance.
2. What did you do this time that you didn't do the other times?
3. Ask yourself, "How did I do that?"
4. Break down that behavior into its subparts.
5. Write down the temporary list of all the steps that made a difference.
6. Can you drop any steps and still get the same result?
7. Write down and keep all the must-have steps.

3. *Collate/Chunk up*

Then I picked up all the good points made by these experts and all those steps that I followed (unconsciously) to give my best performance.

1. Chunk up and sort into very big catch-all categories (areas of concern).
2. Attach solutions to problems.
3. Now chunk down into sub-categories.

4. *Assemble & Assign*

These are the steps for coming out with a complete UBS – imagine the ten parts and 57 sub-parts of the Jet-Set Speaker model (visual, acronyms, alliterations, and numbered). **This is the most tedious step of all.**

1. Associate your specific solution strategies to specific areas of concern for people.
2. For each tactic in a strategy, use a thesaurus for re-word options.
3. Use one of the four different models: Acronym, Alliteration, Numbered, or Visual—or a combination of these.
4. Assign a catchy (but meaningful, not frivolous) name to each specific solution category.
5. Chunk down into tactics or steps to the specific solution strategy.
6. Try to make each strategy (verb) sound like a thing (noun). It should feel like a tangible asset –Framework/Model/ Blueprint/Map/System/Equation/Formula/Quadrant/ Lever/Launchpad/Wagon/Setup etc.

5. *Augment*

Ask yourself

- "What other problems could they (my ideal audience) have?"
- "Once they have implemented my solution, will they succeed?"
- "What else will they need to get an even greater level of success?"
- "Do I have the passion to study and get a solution to the above?"

One final thought on this: When I present my model "Tri-Summit Storytelling System" to corporates, I am easily offered Rs. 1 lakh per hour in India. If I had been speaking the same content without my UBS (the visual + alliteration model), I would have been begging for business. Such is the power of MODELS/ FRAMEWORKS.

REMEMBER: You should not speak/write professionally without having your UBS in place. A UBS will automatically 'augment' your value as a speaker/author. You will be taken much more seriously if you have a UBS in place.

Once your UBS is in place, you must think of the mediums through which you can offer your product. **The best mediums are:**

- A book
- A live seminar/training/workshop/boot-camp
- A video product of your live seminar/training/workshop shared in one of the following three possible ways:
  - Direct shipping of the encrypted physical media to your clients (DVDs/USB Drives etc.). In this, you may buy a security license that makes sure that the contents can't be copied from your media, that the media need to remain inserted whenever you watch these videos, and that the media will run only on one computer. You may also include validity for a particular period. So the question of piracy doesn't arise in this case.
  - Hosting your videos on a secure site and just sharing the username and password with your clients
  - Platform Sales of your video products (or book)

The other **less desirable media** are:

- Studio recordings
- Audio products
- Podcasts
- Webinars
- Blogs

- Newsletters
- Premium coaching (small groups/one-on-one)
- Online marketing

BOOK

If you want to be taken seriously, you must have a published book (in both hard copy and electronic media such as Kindle). It is better to have the book published by a publisher, though self-publishing is extremely easy these days. If you want your other businesses to really multiply in revenue and reach, book-writing is the single most powerful idea. The reasons/advantages of having a published book for an expert are:

- People automatically believe that you are an expert.
- It is very easy to get Speaking Engagements or Corporate Trainings if you are an author.
- It is easy to sell your other solutions (training programs, seminars, video products etc. if you have a published book).
- It is much easier to reach out to many more people through a book.

PLATFORM SALES

If you are asked to speak for 60 to 90 minutes at a platform, you can explain your model in brief by creating such a powerfully compelling future-story (such as 'their life will change forever if they were to get hold of your full solution') that they can't wait to run to the back of the room to buy your stuff (book/videos etc.). In 2013, I managed to sell 427 video-sets of my program **Jet-Set Speaker** from a platform that had an audience of 2300 people and raised a handsome amount of money for the promoters. All my life, I have been selling my workshops/classes/training programs from stage. Selling from stage is an extremely powerful medium when it comes to making money.

Live 2-3-4-5 day training events: This is where you make a lot of your money. Here, you don the role of a trainer and teach your model in much greater depth. The participants in this event are more serious than those in Sales events. These people have already paid you and are willing to learn much more. Once you record these live sessions, you may start selling the videos of the same sessions (for audiences globally) and keep making money even when you are sleeping/vacationing. Just to give you an example, in 2013, I conducted my event called **Life Without A Boss** over three days (Fri-Sun) in collaboration with a Platform Sales Coordinator in London and sold the video products for two of my products **Know The World in 24 Hours** and **The Jet-Set Speaker**.

So, spend some time and create your UBS. Creating different mediums for offering your products will be easy after this.

A word about selling these products

Your products or offers have to move in the form of a staircase:

Free: Reports, White-papers, Sample videos, Cheat-sheets, Quick start guides (downloadable when people fill in the opt-in page on your website).

Low-priced: Book, tickets to a low-priced sales event (1-2 hours) etc.

Medium-priced: Audio products, fragmented video products (one-to-three hour DVDs), ticket to a one- to three-hour live event.

High-priced: Full video solutions, live seminars (2-4 days), recordings of live events.

Premium-priced: One-on-one consulting, Gold memberships, Platinum memberships, Mastermind groups, Inner circles etc. In these models, people have direct access to you (either one-on-one or in very small exclusive groups). This is for the most serious people. This is an insanely lucrative option.

Product formats: There are a few pointers here:

- **Use a noun** (to make it sound tangible): System, Formula, Blueprint etc.
- **Create physical products:** Strange though it sounds, even in the age of the Internet, people like physical products (CDs/DVDs/USB Drives, printed Books etc.)
- **Use really impressive graphics:** High-value graphics create higher perceived value. So get a professional designer. A great graphic may enable you to charge up to ten times for the same product.
- **Create Boxes (physical):** Again the logic working behind this idea is just the same. Package these products beautifully.

The philosophy behind selling these products:

"Before people buy from you, they have to buy into you."

So before selling the product, sell the persona (you will learn about this in the next chapter ***Positioning***). No gimmicks should be used at all. NONE! You end up diluting your persona the moment you resort to gimmicks like these:

- Referrals
- Bonuses
- Discounts
- Deadlines: scarcity – few seats left or few sets left
- Special edition/Limited edition

Because when it comes to life-changing products:

"People buy when they are ready to buy not when you want to sell."

And, even if you are able to attract a few clients by this cattle-class strategy, you will lose in the long run.

Make this a policy:

"I don't want price-shopping clients; I want only value-shopping clients."

One last thought: Don't wait for 10 years to come up with the perfect product or the perfect speech or the perfect book. It will never happen.

In a live-seminar that I attended in the US in 2011, Guy Kawasaki shared what Steve Jobs once told him:

"Real leaders ship."

It has a powerful meaning for you. Think about it.

Where is your product?

$$$$

POSITIONING

At least 90% of your success as a Solopreneur depends on just this one word: Positioning.

Hitler's Brother

Right from a very early age, thanks to my drawing teacher Mr. Bhatti, I had developed a very strong antipathy towards drawing and sketching. I would freak at the very notion of picking up a pencil or a crayon. I hated these subjects so much that I couldn't draw a straight line even with a ruler.

The year was 1991. Like many unfortunate people in India, I too joined Engineering. I was not unhappy as I thought Engineering would at least not involve anything artistic such as drawing or sketching. But on the fourth day, when I saw the time-table, for the first two periods, it read *Engineering Drawing–I*. "WHAT?!"

The Professor (Mr. Mathur) saw me visibly uninterested in the session. He came over to my desk and started: "Do you think you are very smart?" *How can one answer such a loaded question? A 'yes' would have meant being thrown out of the class and a 'no' would have been a clear slap on my existence.* I just sat there, staring at him in utter defiance. He shouted: "You would have never seen any man worse than me. If I want, you will not pass even the first year of your

Engineering in 10 years. So stop all this looking around and pay attention."

Mr. Mathur went back to the stage and said: "Ok class, time for some action now. Take out your rulers, keep them straight, and draw five linear patterns using an **HB** pencil." In one sentence, he had uttered 3 words that I had hated all my life: **Rulers, Straight, and Linear.**

I loathed this man. I immediately had a nickname for him: HB. *Hitler's Brother.*

My strong revulsion for drawing somehow ensured that I couldn't concentrate on anything at all in the first semester. Consequently, as I have mentioned earlier, I failed in all the subjects and I was expelled for six months.

Upon my return to the college, I saw three different reactions from three groups of people in my contact sphere at that time:

- My parents thought that my rebellion would someday kill me. They just advised me to fit in and comply with the teachers.
- My teachers thought that I was a confirmed loser, that I was wasting my time, and that I wasn't meant for something as rigorous as Engineering.
- My friends thought that I was some rock-star; after all, I was the only one earning and footing their beer-bills at that time. One of them even went on to say: "why don't you stay out of the college for a few more years and keep working (and paying our bills)?"

I asked myself. "Although I am the same person, why do these groups of people have such different perceptions about me?" I recollected the most crucial lesson in the book *Positioning*, that I had read a few years ago:

"Perception is the only reality."

It's like, once your family members start believing that you are lazy, even after you have run 10 marathons, they still think you are lazy. Perceptions just don't change.

A huge realization dawned on me: "If I had communicated a single, specific, and crisp message to the world as to who I was, these three groups of people would not have had such different perceptions about me."

Positioning is that single (absolutely laser-sharp) message that defines who you are. What you stand for. What you stand against. Positioning removes the clutter from the mind of the prospect. That day, I sat down to write my Personal Positioning.

Let's step into the world of business. Most of the CEOs of the biggest Fortune-500 companies agree that if you want to develop just one skill for a lifetime, it must be the skill to *sell.* The truth is:

> **"If you are not selling something for profit, you most probably are working for someone who is."**

The biggest challenge in business and in life is *selling*. It could be anything: selling your product, service, idea, vision, cause, or pitching to a VC.

"Life is a series of Sales Situations" – **Patricia Fripp.**

Even when a father tries to convince his child by saying, "Son, I am busy this evening. I will surely play with you tomorrow," he is selling his point. Selling happens not just when an exchange of money is involved. Selling implies **convincing, pitching, influencing, and persuading**. In fact, most meaningful interactions between any two entities entail *'selling'*.

Selling is the purest pursuit. For an employee, *'sales'* equals *'salary'*. 'No sales' equals 'no salary'. The best of companies are written off as dead-ducks if their balance sheets read red. Selling is what makes the world tick. Imagine what changes in a recession: the people remain the same, the products remain the same, and the internal company remains the same. What changes? The only thing that changes is sales. And all hell is let loose. Don't think of selling as a bad word. If you can sell extremely effectively, you are hot-currency in today's world.

But there is an immediate **downside** to this: People hate being sold to.

In this world of information-overload, where at all times someone or the other is trying to sell something to us, we have become so wary of selling that our *sales-filters* are up the moment anyone tries to sell us anything.

So an interesting **paradox** of human existence is: Selling is what makes the world tick but people hate being sold to.

How does one solve this?

The solution: POSITIONING

Positioning is the difference between being able to charge $1,000 for a product and $100,000 for the same product. Surprisingly, people think of positioning as something you do to the product. Here is the myth-buster:

> **Positioning is not what you do to the product; positioning is what you do to the mind of the prospect (buyer).**

Positioning is the art of hijacking the minds of people to such an extent that you never have to sell your product, service, idea, or cause to anyone; **people sell it to themselves.** They become your raving fanatics, your extreme brand advocates. If you want everlasting success, absolutely guaranteed everlasting success, exist in only one place: people's minds. And hijack only one thing: people's minds. Positioning gives you a 10- to 20-year holiday because there is no delete button on the human mind. Once the right perception is created, it just stays.

But remember one thing:

> As a Solopreneur, your Personal Positioning has to be absolutely genuine, heartfelt, and sincere – a true reflection of your personality. Never create a public message that is not

a direct extension of your personality. You have to make sure that you have absolute congruence between what you believe and what you communicate to the external world. There should be no difference between your inner and outer persona.

When "who you are at the very core" is congruent with "your external image", your personal brand becomes naturally magnetic and aspirational.

Positioning is the single, most powerful idea for LIFE.

Some absolutely critical steps for your PERSONAL POSITIONING:

1. Divide people
2. Claim your topic
3. Manage your Personal Online Avatar – Website, YouTube, Facebook

Let's dive in to understand this in detail.

DIVIDE PEOPLE

Are You Lady Gaga? She is the most searched Internet celebrity of the modern era: Lady Gaga. This woman absolutely symbolizes rebellion. At the MTV music awards in 2010, she wore a dress wholly made of raw beef. The entire social media space/ blogosphere went wild with discussions. Lovers and haters in equal numbers! If she hadn't done anything like this, this level of frenzied mania among her fans would have never happened to her brand.

Does everyone agree with her style? No. So the lesson is simple:

Trying to please everyone is the guaranteed road to disaster, and the ultimate sin, in Expert Positioning and Personal Branding.

Instead, you have to do the following:

- Polarize opinions
- Challenge beliefs
- Look for extremes
- Be divisive
- Be very clear as to what you are and what you aren't
- Take a stand – what you stand for and what you stand against
- Be very clear as to who your customer is and who isn't

"NOBODY DISLIKES ME" is a DISASTER: All our lives, we have been advised to look for things that unite us. But to really succeed at the game of positioning, you have to polarize opinions and divide people. In fact, if you try to please everyone, you will never stand out. Because, even if you are God, you will never reach the status: "Everyone likes me." If you are absolutely plain-vanilla, you may definitely reach the status: "No one dislikes me." But this is disastrous for your business.

I have personally used this strategy extremely effectively throughout my career. Let's see a few examples:

- **GMAT-Training** (www.top-one-percent.com): Imagine TOP-ONE-PERCENT as the name of your offering – an extreme example of creating a divide. "Exclusive GMAT-Prep for 99th percentile aspirants! Not for everyone! If you want a score of less than 760, leave this webpage right now." Does every GMAT aspirant like me? NO! Do I want every GMAT aspirant to like me? NO! Am I dividing opinions? YES! Does it make me even more successful? You bet!

  In fact, by saying '99th percentile aspirants only', I am targeting only the top-one-percent customers. Does it mean I am losing the remaining 99 percent customers? NO! Does it mean I am losing at least 50 percent of the customers? YES! So the aforementioned point- look *for extremes* - makes absolute sense. Target the very best and the tipping point will soon tip AND the ordinary will automatically come along. But if I hadn't taken this as my positioning, I would have been fighting for scraps at the bottom 5% of the pyramid.

  - Imagine two scenarios when I pitch my message to a working professional looking to do an MBA: "I want you to study only in the top-10 Business-Schools of the world (Ivy-League or equivalent). I definitely believe that you must target only top-one-percent excellence in whatever you do. And to get into the top-10 Business-Schools, the first step is a high GMAT score. That's why I want you to target only the 99th percentile (top-one-percent) score."

    VERSUS

    "We are the leading GMAT training provider in the country."

- **The Jet-Set Speaker:** "Professional Speaking for global stages, not Public Speaking at weddings, funerals, companies, churches, schools, colleges, or clubs (Toastmasters/Rotary etc.).

  For the first time in India, anyone ever talked about the idea called 'Professional Speaking'. There is a clear division here. All the communication-coaches in the country offer 'Public Speaking'. But I created a completely different category:

Professional Speaking. This is what I blatantly said in my communications: if you have to give a presentation in your company the next week, this is not the course for you.

This course prepares you for global-stages. This is only for those people who want to take up SPEAKING as a full-time career. This is for people who want to earn a fortune through speaking. **This is for the millionaire messenger who wants to make millions while serving millions.** Because of this divide, I am able to get all those who are looking for a 'Professional Speaking' solution. And I am able to heighten their aspirations to a level that they can't stop themselves from joining this course. And the program has been immensely popular.

If you offer a program, imagine how you can use your core beliefs to propagate your core persona. Think about it very carefully. What do you clearly stand for/against? I am sharing some examples of how I have used the 'divide people' strategy while promoting some of my earlier programs. After reading the points below, please write some such points about yourself (whatever you believe in).

- **I believe in exceptional excellence**: Whatever you take up, try to beat the best in the world, not your neighbor, colleague, or friend. I hate mediocrity (people who are happy even if they belong to the middle part of the bell curve). I hate the usual 'cattle-class' existence. So if you find mediocrity seductive, just f*** off. If you are lazy, skeptical, scared, risk-averse, reluctant to learn anything new, complacent, or inefficient, don't even bother to contact me. I am not the right training partner for you. I want only those people who believe in being only in the top-one-percent successful people in the world. People who fall shy of giving absolutely superhuman effort – people who just believe in ***'just getting by'*** in life turn me off no end. I hate people who don't want to do anything to change the status quo even if they know that their lives are completely screwed up.
- **I believe in challenging everything conventional.** People who defy every rule in every rule-book ('Screw-it!', and 'I-don't-care-

even-two-hoots' kind) are the ultimate fascination, to the level of hypnotism and obsession. There are no rules; there are only suckers who are ruled by them. I hate people who believe in any kind of social mores, morals, rules, norms, or regulations—those who believe in anything standard, rational, average, as-per-norms or right.

What is your list of a few such statements that you believe in?

EMBRACE REBELLION

"Observe the masses and do the opposite." – **Walt Disney**

For the last twenty-five years, the most successful example of a Solopreneur has been only one name: Tony Robbins. But when Tony started out in the mid-1980s, the 'healers' industry in America was already choc-a-block with thousands of life-coaches jostling for space. It would have been well-nigh impossible for Tony to make his mark in such a red ocean. What Tony did instead is still considered legendary. He appeared on a Canadian radio channel and openly challenged all the psychologists of the world:

> "All the psychologists of the world are frauds. In just 30 minutes, I can cure any patient suffering from acute-depression that these 'experts' can't cure in even 3 years. These people may have a PhD in psychology. I bloody don't care. I have a PhD in results."

This one statement made Tony the most successful Solopreneur of the modern era. Tony has impacted millions of people across more than a hundred nationalities and created an unparalleled fortune of hundreds of millions of dollars for himself. If Tony Robbins had not taken this rebel stand, he would have been just another NLP practitioner in the US.

People buy into your persona as much as into your solution. The starting point to make someone a raving fanatic must be to share your rebellious beliefs. I am sharing 15 of my beliefs to illustrate how I have positioned myself (the paragraphs below truly epitomize my spirit). After reading the points below, please write some such points about yourself (whatever you believe in).

1. Death to all sacred cows! Sacred cows make the best burgers. I have slain all my sacred cows and made the best burgers out of them.

2. I don't work with my best interests in mind; I work with your best interests in mind. Your success is my success. I have an extremely firm belief that **if you spend enough time with me, I can change your life. Completely!**

3. I want a piece of your mind, not a pound of your flesh: Inherited attributes (physical characteristics, body, looks, skin color, nationality, family background, or inherited wealth) don't excite me. I am interested in something that you didn't inherit in your DNA, something that you acquired after coming into this world (and that's why it is absolutely different, absolutely unique, absolutely you); that thing is your mind. I would be more excited by something that lies outside your résumé.

   More than 99% of the information that people write in their résumés is not unique; someone somewhere will have the same attributes. The best thing I can learn from you is your unique perspectives. And even a Harvard education can't make anyone unique; the same education is shared by thousands of others every year. The only thing unique about you is your perspectives—your convictions, your quirks, your take on life, your thought process, your boldness, your understanding of life from your own lens, your successes and failures, your strengths and weaknesses, your flairs and foibles, your idea of craziness and irrationality, your hobbies and interests, your ecstatic and sad moments, your way of having fun, and everything that makes your persona unique. All I want to do is pick your mind, listen to your unique perspectives, and keep learning. I love to keep myself in "permanent beta". For me, 'finished' is an F-word.

4. My most fundamental belief: *When everyone zigs, you should zag*. Nobody else around the world offers any such programs as I offer. I believe in absolutely unique success-templates. The usual, risk-free, tried-and-tested, and run-of-the-mill (copied) models never excite me. If anyone, anywhere in the world, has already done what I have thought of doing, either I simply bail out or I try to be absolutely unprecedented in the way it is done. That is my Purple Cow. Consequently, I have always enjoyed a competition-free market.

5. Impact has always been my *muse*. Everything that I say or do must create impact. And to create an impact, I must have the deepest convictions about whatever I do. Trying out different business ventures has always given me the necessary kick, adrenaline, and fun. I have never bothered much about the end result. I have never been in any profession that is not an extension of my core persona. If you make your profession an extension of your persona—the amalgamation of your convictions, your belief-system, your deepest passions, and your best skills—the typical byproducts of your passion (money, fame, and success) will start chasing you like a speeding bullet with your name chiseled all over it.

6. I don't respect anyone just because of their age, lineage, pedigree, or background. I respect people for what they personally stand for. I refute the silly idea touted so blatantly in India: that a person's age has anything to do with their maturity levels. I have had great friendships/relationships with people half my age and I have met jackasses twice my age. I can't respect anyone just because they're older. Also, if there is one breed of people that needs the most education in India, it's parents. The right parenting is sorely missing from our society.

7. I am not patriotic. I believe that the best reflection of a society's progress is the completely unquestioned freedom (of all kinds) that women can enjoy without being

answerable or branded; for India, the less said, the better.

8. I don't believe in the idea of competition. I compete only with myself and not with the whole world. I don't want to be better than my competition; I just want to be better than my current self. I love to raise the bar in whatever I do. The restlessness to beat myself just doesn't die.

9. I do not care about what the society thinks of all my unconventional beliefs. I don't believe in complying with any standards that are considered societal/familial norms. My simple philosophy: **You should never explain/justify to others why you do something:** you do those things because you believe in them. The society can go get a life (or death, if it so pleases); I don't care even 2 hoots. I believe in liberation—of thoughts, of action, of mind, of body, of soul—everything. I don't think something is "wrong" only if it is defined by the silly and self-appointed society to be "morally wrong". To hell with such a society! I feel no pangs of conscience in breaking the self-styled moral code imposed by the extremely stupid society around. I believe in my gut. I do crazy and outrageous things simply because they feel right. This philosophy has always worked. I have not, even for a second, regretted any of my choices.

10. I am a very quick decision-maker and am also someone who has nothing to do with either the good or the bad past. I can very quickly forget the bad past as if it never happened. I can easily look ahead. I have never taken even 5 minutes to make various choices in life. All my choices are instantaneous (based on gut, not on data).

11. I think "Education" imparted at most places in India (Schools, Colleges, Universities, Training Centers etc.) is worse than a joke—a complete antithesis of what we need to succeed in life. Most people in India are unemployable, even if they are employed. This explains a risk-averse, non-entrepreneurial nation full of prejudices and mediocrity. We totally lack excellence as a way of life.

12. I am driven by the ability to be creative in every single thing I do. I cannot exist even for 5 minutes in any job/profession that does not let me think out of the box. If I take up a project, I live, talk, and breathe only my project until I am completely satisfied. I am fully (personally, emotionally, and intellectually) invested in the task at hand.

13. I believe that money should be an offshoot of whatever you do and not a driver. The driver must be a purpose larger than yourself – to impact and change lives. I believe in the 10000-hour rule as laid out by Malcolm Gladwell in his book "Outliers". If you genuinely invest 10000 (absolutely dedicated, passionate, and committed) hours of Deliberate Practice in developing a skill, you can surely achieve the "best-in-the-world-at-that-skill" status.

14. Three nouns that describe me perfectly are: Passion, Rebellion, and Wit. Five adjectives that describe me are: Imperfect, Naughty, Crazy, Liberated, and Entrepreneurial. There must be countless funny bones in my body. I can definitely make you LAUGH. I'm fiery, fearless, and fun (in the reverse order).

15. **My life's mission:** To help YOU lead a **Top-One-Percent**, freaking awesome, absolutely insane, and super-kickass life loaded with more money, more time, and more impact.

What is your list of a few such statements that you believe in?

____

____

____

____

____

____

____

____

____

HIT AT THE GUT LEVEL

Build a visceral traction at the fundamental persona level, not at the product level.

It is not rare for people to tattoo the Harley-Davidson logo on their arms. Can you imagine such obsession for your brand?

If you want such brand-fanatics, you need to appeal to people at their fundamental persona level, not at the product (feature/benefit) level.

B.O.L.D. – Beware of Lady Dynamites: The whole plank of the program was rebellion, excellence, and autonomy; right from the name, the content, the attitude—everything was positioned at a persona level, not at the level of product or features. Before starting, I bounced this idea off at least 200 women professionals. Each one of them raved about the concept with dizzying fanaticism, saying that every successful (or wanting to be successful) woman will jump at such a program.

I just didn't sell any feature of the program at all; I sold a future story using two of the most powerful words in communication: IMAGINE and YOU.

This was the positioning for the program:

Imagine a life in which:

1. You are INSANELY PASSIONATE about your work, have all the FUN in the world doing it, and LOVE every moment of it.
2. You are in the top 1% pool in the world at whatever you do (your specific domain).
3. You get extraordinary RECOGNITION for the work you do. You have the feeling of OWNERSHIP for your work and an exceptional sense of BELONGING.
4. You can TALK extremely effectively on ALMOST ANY TOPIC IN THE WORLD because you have the requisite KNOWLEDGE, multi-disciplinary perspectives, and world-class communication skills to OWN THE STAGE.
5. You create a positive IMPACT on people's lives on a daily basis.
6. You earn absolutely satisfactory amount of MONEY and have loads of time to ENJOY that money.
7. You enjoy an enviable monetary, professional, personal, and intellectual GROWTH every month, every quarter, every year.
8. You take your own decisions without seeking anyone's approval or giving any kind of justifications/explanations to anyone at all.
9. You are incredibly bold, fiercely independent, and breathtakingly liberated. The society or the people around you (family, friends etc.) don't influence any of your decisions.
10. You don't have to do things; you choose to do them.

In short, you live life completely on your own terms!

BOLD:

It is not a course;
It is not a product;
It is not a service;
It is not an education;
It is not an experience;
It is not a journey;
It is the best JOYRIDE of your life that you will ever take.

Don't wait for the best JOYRIDE of your life. Just Jump in!

All the participants vouched for the same: the name had something magnetic about it. So appeal at the **gut** LEVEL.

If your business is defined by YOUR personal brand, you can easily hit at the gut level. AND you will find it very easy to position any extensions that come along. But if your positioning is tied to your product or feature, it may be really difficult for you to position any extensions.

A case in point is how Dell's MP3 player (which was much better than the iPod) bombed miserably. For people, Dell was a PC, not a person. But for Apple fanatics, Apple was never a computer. Apple was a symbol of the personal rebellion of Steve Jobs. So anything coming from the Apple arsenal became a hit.

Over the last 18 years, I have done things as different as chalk and cheese. But I never positioned my offerings at the product level. I tied all my offerings to my core persona. So nobody asks me: "You are a GMAT-Trainer. How are you offering the Jet-Set Speaker?"

The reason: I have never sold my product; I have always communicated my deepest beliefs.

CLAIM YOUR TOPIC

Once again, you don't need any degrees or qualifications to claim your topic.

What should be your topic? Here are some of the hottest topics (among the many hundreds) that you may consider depending on your level of expertise:

1. Motivation/Attitude/Success mindset
2. Relationships
3. Leadership
4. Spirituality
5. Investing
6. Style and fashion
7. Business growth
8. Productivity (time management etc.)
9. People management (teamwork etc.)
10. Health/fitness/wellness
11. Marketing, Branding, Positioning, Digital Marketing
12. Social Media
13. Sales/Persuasion
14. Parenting
15. Entrepreneurship
16. Solopreneurship
17. Brain science
18. Storytelling
19. Knowledge/Perspectives
20. Speaking/Presentation

What is going to be your topic? ____________________

____

____

____

Use the words "The ONLY" ...... "Expert in ......"

Don't use the word 'best' in your positioning. Imagine this:

"We are one of the **best** providers of all kinds of accounting services in the city." It sounds insincere and lame.

Your answer: The ONLY ______________________ Expert in ________________.

Use 'author of'/'founder of'/'creator of'

If possible, use at least two of the three. So I can say:

> "Hi, I am Sandeep Gupta, author of the book Million Dollar Solopreneur, Founder of Your-First-Million-Dollars, and creator of the B.O.L.D. program – Beware of Lady Dynamites."

Your answer: Hi, I am ______________________, author of the book ______________________, Founder of ______________________, and creator of the program ______________________.

Claim something massive/Make a very bold promise

Don't be scared here. In the past, I have claimed some of the boldest results. For example:

> "In 24 hours, you will learn more about life-success than what a 24-month MBA from Harvard can teach you."

> "In the next 2 days, you will learn more practical marketing than what a 2-year MBA from Kellogg can teach you."

On my Million Dollar Solopreneur website (www.MillionDollarSolopreneur.com), this is what I claim: "Ensure complete financial freedom in just 12 months."

Another example is on my website www.top-one-percent.com

"If you find any other GMAT Test-Prep Company (or any other GMAT Trainer) even one-tenth as good, go and join there."

Your massive claim/bold promise: ____________________

____

____

Check the next page for the website screenshot.

Home Screenshot for www.Top-One-Percent.com

MANAGE YOUR PERSONAL ONLINE AVATAR

You must be found online. Remember, in today's times, people will Google you before they do business with you. So you have to make sure you have a strong online presence.

You need to be "perceived" as an EXPERT in your niche because people pay more for context than for content. To this effect, create a superbly designed, sleek website. Even if you are just starting out, your website doesn't have to imply that you are just starting out.

Check the website below:

The website makes you believe that this person is a thorough professional and that he can definitely help you with your property-investing needs.

And now check the following picture of a firm that has much more experience in dealing with what Paul Stebles is offering.

Whom are likely to trust more? Paul Stebles or By Abacus?

The following must be part of your online presence:

1. Your Picture on your website
2. Your Story (your Personal Journey)
3. Active Groups/Forums (Facebook/Twitter)
4. Your Videos (speaking to a live audience)
5. Client Testimonials (preferably videos)

Your Picture: It goes without saying but you must have a picture of yours (preferably YOU speaking to a LIVE audience) shared on your website.

Your Story (Your Personal Journey): Your life story positions you as an expert in your claimed topic. Your Personal Journey is an integral part of The Solopreneur Blueprint. The picture below shows one of my blogs with my life-story.

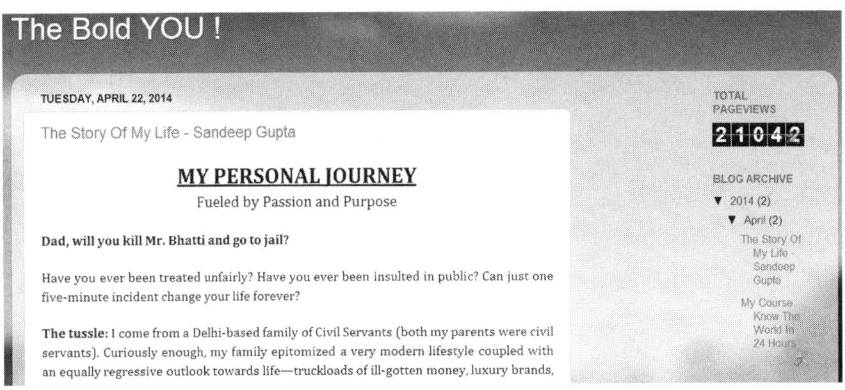

Active Groups/Forums (Facebook): It is extremely important to keep a vibrant Facebook community (remember this: you may be on Twitter, but all your followers may not be on Twitter. So, Facebook is a better medium for active discussions. The picture below shows one of my thousands of such posts and the activeness of the forum.

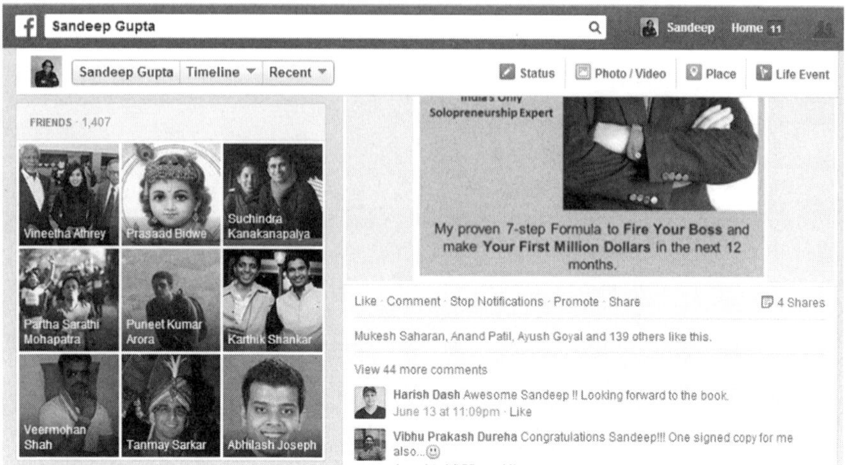

Your Videos (speaking to a live audience): There is no better proof than a LIVE-session video. So if ever you get an opportunity to present somewhere, ***do record yourself without fail***. Two of my live videos have generated a lot of extra revenues in just the last one year. The pictures below show me in such LIVE sessions.

Client Testimonials (preferably videos): There is no better closure than sincere, heartfelt and raving client testimonials. For obvious reasons, videos work best for testimonials.

On all these mediums, ask yourself this question: Is my MESSAGE so powerful that people will open their hearts and wallets for my idea? Will they be BLOWN AWAY? I want this feedback for all your sessions: "I was BLOWN AWAY."I can't even begin to tell you how many times I have received such feedback from my participants. In essence, *tap into EMOTIONS, not logic.*

EMOTIONS: a participant in my Million Dollar Solopreneur seminar once asked me: "You say: Sell to the emotional brain. So, what, according to you, is the best emotion to arouse in people?"

This question made me think for six long months. I studied 1000 most successful print/video advertisements of all time. The answer was glaringly obvious: the best emotion to arouse is **AWE**. The kind you feel when you gape down the bottomless gorge of The Grand Canyon and marvel at the very potency of Nature. **That feeling is sheer AWE.** Nothing else makes such an impact on people as the feeling of AWE.

Self-development or Shelf-development?

Have you ever purchased something that you didn't need? That you didn't use later?

Well, you are not alone. My parents did so all the time. I grew up in a family where my parents purchased things for no logical reason, especially books—and I always wondered: "why should you buy something that you never use?"

If you had been with me in my drawing room when I was 8, you would have seen 3 gigantic bookshelves overflowing with books—big hardcover volumes from all parts of the globe. *Russian Revolution, Capital Punishment Systems of the Last 1000 Years, World Wars, Occult Sciences, Philosophy, Religion, Economics, Law* – the works. The shelves were opened only for one purpose: cleaning.

Whenever the shelves were opened, some books invariably fell down and landed 'thud' on the floor with the smell of dust. I once asked my father, "Dad, why do you buy so many books when I never see you reading?" I could see him becoming really uncomfortable with such questions. He said, "It is for self-development." I retorted, "But I don't ever see you reading. Dad, this is not self-development; this is SHELF development."

My dad was very possessive about his books. I was not allowed to touch the books. He even had a label on each of the shelves: "Don't touch without permission." For me, those books were some kind of forbidden fruit. Naturally, I got more and more intrigued. When one day my parents were out at work, a servant (Mahipal Singh Choudhary from Haryana) was cleaning the shelves. A particular volume of Grolier Encyclopedia just tumbled out and fell down. I picked up the book, and, the moment I opened the book, I got hooked to it. Volume 17: *Countries of the World*. The pictures fascinated me no end. And our servant panicked.

> *"Bettaji kitab vapas de do ... saabji meri khaal kheench lenge." (Young master, please keep the book back or else Master will skin me!)*

I requested him to let me look at the book for some time, and somehow with great stress on his face, he allowed me to read the book.

> *"Saabji ke aane ke pahle vapas rakh dena."*
> *(Please keep it back before Master arrives.)*

I got so hooked that I put a stool and took out all the 22 volumes one by one and just kept on looking at the pictures. By evening, I had turned over all the 22 volumes.

When my dad came back that evening, I just jumped to tell him the joy of having seen the encyclopedia.

"Dad, you should read. These books are very interesting."

He saw me with all the books on the floor, AND without thinking at all, **slapped me** hard.

Dad (fuming and screaming): *"Mahipal, tune naukri karni hai ya nahi? Kisse pooch ke kitaab nikal kar di?" (Mahipal, seems like you don't want a job? Who did you ask before handing the books over?)*

Mahipal: *"saabji bhale hi aap naukri se nikal do par main ek baat zaroor kahoonga ... mere hisab se to bettaji ne koi galti nahi ki hai ... kitaabe to dhool kha rahi hain ... main to chahta hoon ki mera beta padhe ... par hamare paas aise saadhan kahan? Aapka beta padnha chahta hai ... uske paas poori kitaab ki dukan hai ... aur aap use padhne se rok rahe ho?"*

(Respected Master, even if you fire me after this, I will say; the young master has not done anything wrong. The books are gathering dust. It is so ironical, that I want my son to read, but have no means to provide him with such books; your son wants to read, has a whole store full of books, but you are stopping him from reading!)

Dad: *"Mahipal, ab tu mujhe samjhayega ki mujhe apne bachche ki parwarish kaise karni chahiye?"*
(Am I going to learn how to take care of my children from you, a servant Mahipal!)

In the meanwhile my mother also reached home.

Mom (completely puzzled): *"What happened?"*

She remained shocked for some time. When the penny eventually dropped, she gave an almost menacing look to my dad.

Dad: *"Now the servants of the house will tell me what I should do and how I should raise my child."*

Mom: *"Mahipal is absolutely right. What kind of a dad are you? Other kids are beaten for not studying. You must be the only father in the world who is beating his child because he is interested in reading/studying. Rather you must be proud that at such a young age, he is being fascinated by books."*

This hit him hard; he just plonked on the sofa silently, hanging his head in utter bemusement. After about 10 minutes, he got up and said *"sorry"* to all three of us.

Later he said to my mom: *"I was angry not because he read the books but because my orders had been violated. And in the heat of the moment, I ended up slapping my son who wanted to read and study. Shame on me!"*

Logically there was no reason for my dad to slap me but he still did.

Whenever I remember this day, this belief gets reinforced: *We always act emotionally (irrationally) before we act logically (rationally).*

Surprising as it may sound, but human decision-making is a

completely irrational process, be it my dad deciding to slap me or your client deciding to buy your product and services from you. Let's understand this process in some detail.

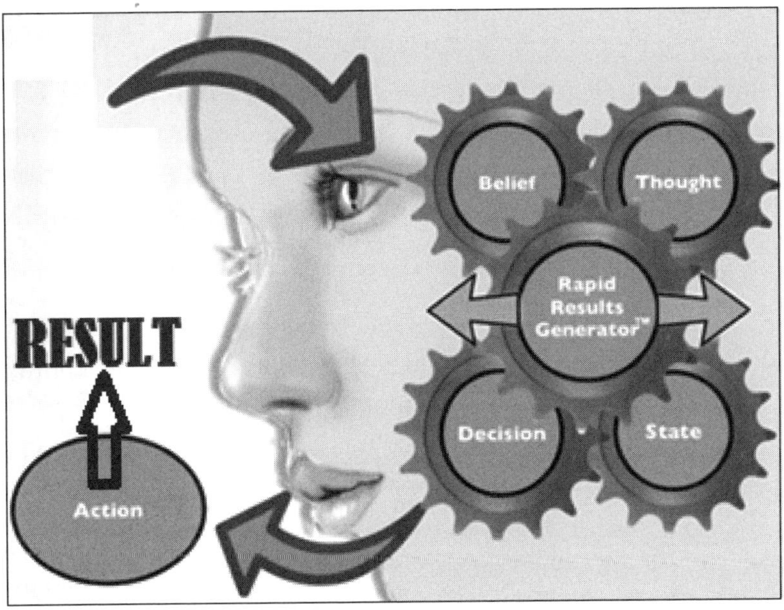

Let's start with a few simple questions:

Q: What change do your clients want?
A: They want a different RESULT in their lives, careers, or businesses.

Q: How can they get a different result?
A: They have to take a different ACTION.

Q: How can they take a different action?
A: They have to take a different DECISION.

Q: How can they take a different decision?
A: They need to be in a different STATE.

Q: How can they be in a different state?
A: They need to have different THOUGHTS.

Q: How can they have different thoughts?
A: They need to have different BELIEFS.

So this is how the whole cycle works:

Beliefs → Thoughts → State → Decisions → Actions → Results

90% of your job as a Speaker, Author, Trainer, or Consultant is always to change people's **beliefs** so strongly that the remaining five are automatically taken care of. Imagine yourself at an Apple store. You see the latest gizmo from the company and you just WANT IT—PERIOD! This irresistible desire is the **belief** (emotion). This will translate into the **thought** (you will tell yourself a future story that it will be 'cool' to have that gizmo. This will send you into a different mental **state** (happiness at the very thought of possessing it). The state will get you to **decide** to buy. The next thing is that you swipe your card and buy the gadget. This is **action**.

The action may lead to a different **result** in your life (Imagine you are in a flight and are seated next to a man/woman having the exact same gadget. Because of the same gadget, you may strike up a conversation and one thing may lead to another. You may even end up being business partners.

But what is the seller's (company's) role here? It just needs to arouse such a strong and irresistible desire in you that the other five steps are automatically taken care of.

In the same way, your job as a Solopreneur is to arouse such an attraction in your solution that the rest of the steps are automatically taken care of. In other words, you don't have to sell anything to them; they will sell your solution to themselves.

Emotions create the movement required to drive your customers forward in the buying process. **And nothing creates stronger emotions than your own personal belief system or your story.** Both these POSITION you in their minds indelibly.

The moral of the story: write your personal positioning. TODAY! 90% of your success as a Solopreneur depends on just one word: POSITIONING.

$$$$$

PUBLISHING YOUR CONTENT

Did I hear you right, Charu?

I am not really a proponent of the law-of-attraction ('want something so badly that the universe will conspire to give it to you' or 'when the student is ready the master will appear') kind of theories but what happened in April 2014 was nothing short of validation for such 'babble'. I placed a regular advertisement in *The Times of India* for my GMAT sessions in New Delhi. A 'studies-abroad' consultant, Charushilla Narula, the literary consultant and Chief Editorial Coordinator for this book, saw the ad and came to discuss possibilities for an association with me. And what followed was absolutely UNREAL.

On 26th April, Saturday, I had my workshop in 3 slots. I could meet Charu for no more 5 minutes (between two slots and amid a lot of frenzy). But, as luck would have it, I asked her to take a copy of the booklet from my previous workshop (it happened to be lying on the table) with her. That was it!

After reading some details about me and my career-journey in the booklet, some chord struck. Charu asked me to write a book (did I hear you right, Charu?) about my Solopreneurship journey. Funnily enough, at least 1000 people had asked me to write a book before this but somehow it didn't 'register'. But in that single moment, something overpowered me. COMPLETELY!

What happened in the next two weeks surpassed the level of all my previous obsessions. Writing this book was such a cathartic journey that I completely lost my sense of space and time. For hours together, I wouldn't register where I was sitting or whether it was night or day. It was BLISS! This entire book was written in just two weeks (it seems that the book just wrote itself). Although I had published a huge amount of content all my life, a book had waited just too long.

What about your content?

As a successful Solopreneur, you will need to continually keep churning out newer and newer content. So let's look at what content you can come out with on a regular basis and how to prepare and package that content:

- Your book
- Your blogs/newsletters/articles/reports/participation in discussion forums
- Promotions through teaching/sales videos (usually shot in a studio)
- Your clients' video testimonials
- Your live-performance recordings (snippets)
- Your interviews (you interviewing other experts/other experts interviewing you)
- Your website content
- Your email promotions

Whatever you offer, add a lot of value in your content. Teach people to the tune of 25% free using any/all the mediums. Then you can surely say: "If you want to learn more, you may consider my comprehensive program XYZ, which teaches this in much greater detail."

People must say: "If s/he can offer such unimaginable, breath-takingly great value without even charging anything, imagine what s/he would offer in his/her actual product!" They should sell your solution to themselves. You can't do a job that is just about passable. I got this feedback from a student:

> "I can't imagine listening to even Obama for 2 full days. But in your 2-day session, I didn't even have moments when my concentration was off. I was blown away."

Once I have won the trust of this person, if and when she needs anything that I am offering in the future, I won't have to sell anything to her; she will sell my products to herself. If by spending tons of money, your client can get X amount of value from someone else, you must be willing to provide her 10X free—AND you are sorted for life; money will chase you like a bullet.

Let's see the purpose of various types of mediums for your content:

Your Book

You must consider writing a book. The entire book-writing and book-publishing process is beyond the scope of this book, but just to give you a little secret, I run a program called 'My First Book', which covers the entire book-writing process (concept, story, content, models, UBS, writing, editing, and publishing) in great detail.

Your blogs/newsletters/articles/reports/participation in discussion forums: Funny as it may sound, the purpose of all these things is just one:

> *Let Google find you and offer you to your prospective clients.*

The more number of times your name appears on various websites, the more likely you will be found in Google Search. So make sure you keep churning out such content for various websites. But don't forget the fundamental tenet: ADD VALUE and TEACH. Don't blatantly sell.

Promotions through teaching videos (usually shot in a studio): surprising though it sounds, YouTube is the second biggest Search Engine in the world. So the more the number of videos you have on YouTube with your name, the more the chances that your actual video will pop up in the first few results on the first page of Google search.

Make sure you add immense value through these videos. The best thing is to teach people something of so much value that they are automatically tempted to buy your solution.

Your Clients' Video Testimonials

From a Sales standpoint, these serve the best purpose. Make sure the feedback videos you upload are absolutely emotional in nature. Stay as far away from logic as possible. People don't open their wallets when they feel they need your solution (logically); they open their wallets when they are *moved* to buy from you. And emotion is the only thing that moves people.

Your Live-performance Recordings (Snippets)

If you want speaking engagements to come to you by the dozens every day, you must have snippets of your LIVE performances in which the audience is also seen. There is no bigger proof for your clients (both B2B and B2C) than your live videos.

I have also seen one strange thing here: even if you offer something serious and mission-critical, your videos in which you make your audience roar into a laughter will always be appreciated more than anything serious that you might ever share. So learn to be natural, confident, and funny on stage.

Your interviews (you interviewing other experts/other experts interviewing you):

One of the best ways to market yourself extremely effectively is to interview other Solopreneurs and be interviewed by them. When others promote you, it sounds much more credible to their audiences.

This comes across as incredibly genuine; ask some questions and lead the interviewee to share their success-story.

You may check a sample here:

https://www.youtube.com/watch?v=WkdW8o0WtqE

Your website content: I find most websites in the world equivalent to a suicide-attempt at selling. Atrocious!

What should your website (make sure it is .com, not any other domain) contain?

- **A custom banner** (graphical header): this gives a sleek and professional look.
- **A strapline (promise):**
  - Start with an action verb
  - Describe the goal or outcome
  - Mention the method to achieve it
  - Include the target audience

  Some examples of promises:
    * Helping you create wealth with commodity trading
    * Creating a laptop lifestyle for time and money freedom
    * Increasing profits for SMEs through strategic marketing
    * Creating dream lifestyles for ambitious Mumpreneurs
- **A very bold promise** – use the word "YOU" as much as possible. Avoid using the word "I" or "WE" as much as possible. Convert every "WE offer" to "YOU get".
- **A grabber:** a piece that completely shocks/awes people.
- **"Earn the right" element**:
  - Who are you?

  - How long have you been doing this?
  - How many people have you helped?
  - What results have you achieved for them?

- **About me/a small informal message from you:** Here you should talk about: "Hi, I am ... author of/founder of/creator of" ... and your claim to fame. An auto-start video of yours introducing yourself (speaking to the camera) may also help here.
- **An opt-in element:** You must get people's first name, last name, email ID, and, if possible, phone number. But you must offer them something in return. So, you must have an opt-in element saying: to download my secrets to XYZ, please fill in your details here.
- As discussed in the chapter on Positioning, your website must contain (1) your live-performance picture, (2) your content videos, and (3) your client testimonial videos.
- **Your book description:** You must have the description of your book, if any, on your website. It lends an unbelievable amount of credibility.
- **Links to Your Social Profiles:** Facebook/YouTube/Twitter etc.
- **Your products/offers:** Don't offer too many features/details; rather present a compelling future story about what may happen if they do own your solution(s). An element of *contrast* (where they are without your solution versus where they can be with your solution) helps immensely.
- **Link to your story (on your blog):** You must have the link to your written story. A well-written story connects with your audience really strongly. If you have a video story, it must be a THEN-NOW-HOW story.
- **The usual:** A call to action/contact and payment options/ shopping cart etc.

You must hire a digital marketing / SEO expert to help you optimize your entire web presence; it helps a lot. Also, get your website professionally designed to give it a sleek look.

Your email promotions: Again, the purpose of this exercise is to add tremendous value and subtly offer them your solutions/video products/books/upcoming workshops/training programs etc. You must provide such tremendous value in these communications that people don't want to unsubscribe from your list (you must give them the option, though). The entire communication must be directed at "YOU GET", not at "I GIVE" or "I AM". In each communication, add a video, if possible.

Remember, your published content is your signature. Invest a lot of time developing it. And keep investing time. Novelty is the name of the game for the Million Dollar Solopreneur. Your content will speak to the world before you will. It has to win people over. Completely!

$$$$$$

PROFESSIONAL SPEAKING

The profession that can make you the maximum money per hour among all professions in the world.

"Sandeep, I could have paid you a hundred dollars for every word you had NOT spoken." —My client after my sales presentation in 2002.

This incident happened just a few weeks before I saw Tony Robbins live in action. I bombed miserably in my presentation because I had left my partner (Kanika) in a state of horrific depression. It was as difficult as juggling chainsaws while walking a tightrope. And Tony cured her depression in just five minutes.

I saw people coming to Tony's seminar from the UK, South Africa, Australia, India, Spain, and almost all other parts of the world. And I went into a self-talk mode.

> "What a shame all these people have to come all the way to America to get this! Why isn't something like this more readily available everywhere in the world? Why do only a few people get this man's help and others are administered drugs by psychiatrists?"

At the end of the seminar, Robbins did an exercise. He asked us to pair up with a stranger. The idea was to get together with one person, sit cross-legged, and look directly into his or her eyes, and send him/her all the presence, love, and connectivity for a few moments.

And here I was: trying to find a partner but no one seemed to want to partner with me. I looked in their direction and I saw people looking away from me. But as Robbins says, there is no failure – only feedback.

The feedback I took was: "These people weren't meant to be my partner. I will go and partner with Anthony Robbins himself." There were 5000 participants and 20 security guards spread throughout the room. I found one guard a bit distracted on his walkie-talkie. In that moment, I waved to Robbins hinting: "Would you be my partner?" I knew that he remembered that I was the partner of the person he had helped. To my great surprise, he agreed.

In that moment, I got my 2 minutes of intimacy with Anthony Robbins that totally changed my life. I felt so much gratitude towards him for bringing my partner back to her feisty self in a matter of just five minutes. I felt a complete sense of gratitude for the skill, the dedication, and the marketing prowess he had. His marketing message had the power to get me to fly to that room and to change my life.

I realized that I wasn't there just for her but also for myself. There had to be something for the victim's supporter in this situation, not just for the victim. Tears welled up in my eyes and somehow my tears connected back to him—he was crying too! It was the biggest moment for me. Like Tony Robbins, I had to be a Professional Speaker.

Back to You

To get to wherever you want to go in life, you need a vehicle. And that vehicle must be a skill—a skill that is extremely rare. If you possess a rare skill, your value as a person goes up extraordinarily. If you can do something that only very few people can do and scale it up to reach out to the whole world, it stands to reason that you are going to get much more recognition and income.

That skill is "The Art of Professional Speaking" – a skill that, if mastered, can increase your income up to a hundred times (with loads of free time at hand). This is the skill of The Millionaire Messenger, someone who can transform people from "fed-up" to "fired-up", impact them, and eventually change them for the better.

So ask yourself:

- "Do I dream of jet-setting the world spreading my message, impacting lives, and earning millions?"
- "For starters, do I want to make the same amount of money as my current monthly income in just 60-90 minutes?"

There is a 20-point process that you can follow to cut into this space. I call it the **Millionaire Messenger Matrix**.

Let's look at all the steps in some detail:

1. **Claim your topic:** We have already discussed this in great detail earlier. You need to claim a topic with the words ONLY .... EXPERT in ....

   So what topic are you claiming?

2. **Choose your audience:** You must be very clear as to who your ideal audience is and who isn't. Many speakers target everyone. This is disastrous. Let's say I am offering the program ***Million-Dollar Solopreneur***. I need to be very clear as to who my customers are and who aren't.

   - People who are already running a brick-and-mortar kind of established business (e.g., a restaurant) aren't likely to be my customers.
   - People who want to remain in jobs aren't likely to be my customers.
   - College students aren't likely to be my customers.
   - People who want to work in the manufacturing sector (or heavy industry) are not going to be my likely customers.
   - Corporates are never going to be my customers (for this program).

   But a large number of high-fliers between 25 and 40 years of age who work in the high-end value segment (Education & Training, Leadership, Marketing, Sales, Communication, Writing, Advertising, IT, Software, Specialized Services etc.) and who feel that they can add value by training/premium coaching/speaking/writing/online marketing/consulting etc. and want to make a fortune—are my ideal customers. Also business-owners in the value-creation segment are my ideal customers.

   So, clearly write down as to who your customers are and who aren't. This will help tremendously.

3. **Collate their problems**: As a Professional Speaker, your job is to take your audiance away from a problem and towards a payoff. You are essentially a healer. So you have to claim a topic and really go in-depth to understand all their problems at an individual level. If you know the current and future needs of your clients, it is extremely easy to design your solutions. Some examples are given below:

Problem	**to**	**Payoff**
Obscurity	to	Celebrity
Insecurity	to	Security
Stagnation	to	Motivation/Growth
I HATE MY WORK	to	I LOVE MY WORK
Powerlessness	to	Autonomy
Loser's mindset	to	Winner's mindset
Fear of speaking	to	Love for speaking
Losing (Business)	to	Winning (Sales)
Employee	to	Boss (Leadership)
Fat	to	Fit
Low productivity	to	High productivity
Old	to	New (Technology/Strategy)
Financial Instability	to	Financial Freedom
S.T.U.C.K.	to	S.T.A.R. (Relationships, Work etc.)
Fed up	to	Fired up
Mess	to	Magic
Frustrated	to	Motivated
Loneliness	to	Belonging
Boredom	to	Excitement
Free	to	Fee
Bad Boss	to	Great Leader
Ignorant	to	Informed
Chump	to	Champ
Failure	to	Success
Employee	to	Entrepreneur
Lousy Presenter	to	World-class storyteller
Life lacks meaning	to	Life has Meaning
Sulking	to	Scintillating

Have-to-do	to	Love-to-do
Used-to-be	to	Yet-to-be
Lackluster	to	Blockbuster
Mess	to	Magic
PASSION	to	PROFITS
Pain	**to**	**Gain**

4. **Craft your story**: We have already discussed this in the chapter on Personal Journey. You must write your story. If you can craft a compelling story, you will see at least 10 times the business coming your way. Such is the power of a great story.

5. **Chart Solution Map**: This step is the same as creating your UBS (discussed in the chapter on Product).

6. **Chunk Your Content**: While delivering a speech, you can't ramble your way through. You have to really organize your content into 10-12 minute pieces that follow a very tight structure.

7. **Chop the Clutter**: There is a saying in the Speaking world: "Great speeches or jokes aren't written; they are rewritten." Don't write a new speech. Make your existing speech better; keep removing the boring bits. **Make sure that there is nothing BORING in your speech.** So when in doubt whether to keep a piece of content or not, it is best to leave it out.

    - Seinfeld will take up to six hours to turn a 9-word joke to a 6-word joke. He says: "My best ad-libs take 8 hours to write."

8. **Change their beliefs:** As a Professional Speaker, you are in the business of CHANGE. If at the end of your presentation, your audience feels: "I need to change something about my life, career, or business", you have earned full marks as a Professional Speaker.

Change Three Types of Beliefs

Beliefs about ABILITY: After attending your program, if a participant (who was absolutely scared to speak on stage) says:

"I can be a Professional Speaker, I can speak for hours, and I am going to start right away"—you have changed their belief change about their ABILITY.

What beliefs about ability can you change for your audience members?

Beliefs about IDENTITY: After attending "B.O.L.D. – Beware of Lady Dynamites" – my program for women Solopreneurs, a participant, who had spent her entire career (more than 15 years) in Information Technology Consulting, realized that she didn't belong there. Within a month she resigned and started her own business. This is a belief-change about IDENTITY.

What beliefs about identity can you change for your audience members?

Beliefs about THE WORLD: After attending "Know the World in 24 Hours", a participant's entire worldview (about a myriad aspects) changed fundamentally, bringing out a massive change in the way she related to the world, interacted with people, and understood the complexity around her. She ended up discussing something that she had learnt in this program with the Sales Head of a Fortune 100 company and blew him away with her uniquely novel perspectives. She was immediately offered a job that she would have died for—at triple her salary. This is a belief-change about the world.

What beliefs about the world can you change for your audience members?

How to Change Beliefs?

You definitely have to do the following:

- Upset
- Divide
- Challenge
- ATTACK what is (the old world)
- INSTALL what can be (new possibilities)

Now remember Tony Robbins calling all the psychologists of the world "frauds".

- Did he upset people? YES
- Did he divide/polarize people? YES
- Did he challenge old beliefs? YES
- Did he attack the old world (*depression takes years to cure*)? YES
- Did he install new possibilities (*any depression can be cured in just 30 minutes*)? HELL, YES!

9. **Charm with Commonality:** Commonality is the key to connection. Don't ever try to be perfect as a Professional Speaker. Either the audience will try to find chinks in your armor, or worse, the audience will think you are special. Being considered special is the WORST thing that can happen to you as a speaker. If they think you are special, they will never connect with you. They will mentally tune you out. They won't take any action on your message. So be imperfect, be human, and be vulnerable.

   Your message should always be: "Look I am not special. But in the journey of life, from some wonderful people I learnt some wonderful things that I would love to share with you so that you can shorten your learning curve. I am someone who was struggling to get by in life at some point in time but I changed. You can, too."

   Share your Five F's: Failures, Flaws, Firsts, Frustrations, and Fuckups. They will just love you as a speaker.

   The irony of the business of speaking is: the most difficult part for people while on stage is 'being themselves'.

   If you try to come across as perfect, you will turn people off.

10. **Connect the Dots:** I did talk about this at length in the chapter on Perspectives. The importance of "connecting-the-dots" can't be overemphasized. Let's say you are to deliver a talk on Storytelling. And you randomly ask a question: "Despite being so frail and feeble compared to so many animals, why do human

beings dominate this planet?" And after a good interaction with the audience, you give the answer that proves to be the most AWE-inducing (WOWWWWWWW!!!!) thing that they have ever heard, and then tie the whole idea back to storytelling, people will not be able to forget you in YEARS.

In a typical 90-minute speech, if you can give your audience 2 such absolutely WOW! moments, they would want to spend the rest of their lives with you.

So think about this: "What 'connect-the-dots' moments would I like to give my audience?"

11. **Create an experience:** Some comments by participants that assure you that you certainly created an experience for them:

    1. I felt as if I watched the best movie of my life for the last 2 days.
    2. I'm always thinking about work, deadline, project, boss, traffic, kids, spouse, EMIs, bills ... what have you. In the last 8 years, it was the first time that I got a chance to talk to myself for two full days (this feedback when the person was sitting among 4000 people).
    3. 10,000 books, 1000 people, 1000 places, and 1000 videos can't give you the perspectives that he has given in just 24 hours.
    4. I have learnt more in the last 3 days than have in the last 5 years.
    5. What I learnt in the last 3 days is more than what I learnt at my IIT (college) in the entire 4 years.
    6. Perhaps he is the only person whom I can name alongside Steve Jobs.
    7. I haven't ever had so many dots connected in my whole life as I have had in the last 3 days.
    8. I have a desire to live longer only to speak. I am ready to give 90 million hours of speech.

9. Among 1000+ people, I felt that he was talking only to me all the time.

10. It is great to have lived in a generation that is able to be a part of his programs.

I want your feedback to beat each of the 10 snippets given above.

What makes people say such unimaginable things? Well, give them an experience that they can't ever forget. Give them such a super-charged emotional journey that they are transported into a trance-like, hypnotic state. To give them such an experience, you have to make them T.A.L.L. (Think, Act, Laugh, and Learn).

THINK: As you talk, you have to make people think. There are two powerful ways to make people think. One: *create an internal dialog*: For example: "I need to change something about my life." Two: *Create pictures in their minds* (about their future story): "With his/her solution in my hands, I am absolutely confident that I can change my life."

ACT: How to make people act on your message? Only one answer: extreme belief change. Their entire identity must be shaken as they listen to you.

LAUGH: If you can't make people laugh, you are going to find it extremely difficult to keep them engaged for even a few minutes at a stretch. In today's Internet-enabled, smartphone era, when people are more interested in WhatsApp than 'What's on', attention spans are at an all-time low. You have to do something all the time to change their state. Laughter is one of the most potent weapons to change their state.

LEARN: Every minute they should feel that they heard something that they couldn't have imagined in their entire lifetimes. Your content must totally shock and awe them. They should feel like shocking thousands of people using what they learn from you. The content must be absolutely novel, gripping, and AWE-inducing.

12. **Charge them up:** Throughout your speech, if they feel: "I need to change something about my life and I am going to do it right away. I am just waiting to jump out of my chair and implement all that I have learnt here," you have truly charged them up. They will buy any solution from you. Because remember this: **the best motivational speaker in the room is not YOU** (the speaker); it is your audience (the listener). And the best way to charge them up is never to shout or to give them a motivational pep-talk or to make them shout; the best way to do so is to send them in a deep **reflection** mode such as: "What am I doing with my life?"

13. **Charter a path:** If your talk is all rah-rah motivation but no tools, they will definitely not feel a sense of accomplishment. So you have to give them lots of tangibles. Even this 20-point Millionaire Messenger Matrix (that we are discussing) is an excellent example of chartering a path. In a single visual, this gives an absolute newbie all the steps required to become a millionaire messenger.

14. **Confine your positioning**: We have already talked about this at length in the chapter on Positioning. You have to define who your customer is and who isn't; what you stand for and what you stand against. So you have to truly confine your NICHE. You have to polarize opinions.

15. **Capture your leads**: Once you put up a website, every lead that you generate is absolutely priceless. So make sure you have a system in place that can capture all the leads (email IDs/phone numbers etc.). Soon you may have a mailing list of thousands of people.

16. **Cultivate a community:** You need to have a vibrant community on Facebook/Twitter/YouTube, which can very easily be integrated into your website. Keep it alive by posting interesting content, especially promotional (value) videos.

17. **Campaign and sell:** Whenever you come up with a new event, program, product, or book, you need to campaign (email, social

media) to your list (loyal audience) with a series of value communications. The call to action must be only after teaching them at least 25% of the content FREE.

18. **Collaborate and Grow:** Find out whosoever is doing similar work and offer to speak at their events absolutely free. You will soon see your business grow really fast.

19. **Cascade your offers:** You must have a ***Strategic Product Staircase***, not just one product.

    Example: First, I started a program on Speaking Skills. Once my clients attended the program, they felt that they needed help with establishing their business of speaking. So I offered A.P.P.E.A.L. – Adorable Personal Positioning Exuded All Life. Next they felt that their content was seriously hampered by their lack of knowledge and perspectives. So, I offered "Know the World in 24 Hours".

    Next when they felt that they needed help with Storytelling/ Story-Writing Skills, I offered Tri-Summit Storytelling System. Next if they wanted to know how to write a book, I offered a solution for that as well (Kick-S.T.A.R.T. Content Creator). Next, when they wanted help on designing their products, I offered CYUBS (Creating Your Unique Branded Solution).

    Next, after having all the attributes, when they wanted to brand themselves, I offered N.E.U.R.O.-Seduction. Next, when all these courses were individually finessed, I started offering Million Dollar Solopreneur as a complete start-to-finish Blueprint. I call it a **strategic-product-staircase** because if you can offer solutions at each step (as and when your clients face more and more obstacles), you are automatically creating an absolutely fanatic buying audience.

    Think of how many products you can offer that can be part of a strategic staircase. If you can, you will have no dearth of repeat customers.

20. **Capitalize your brand:** If you do a fabulous job, the demand

for your products goes global in no time. And because you can't be everywhere in the world delivering your seminars, you must create your video products and keep earning even while you are sleeping.

Why leave any money on the table for others?

Invest in the skill of Professional Speaking. The returns are disproportionate to the amount of effort spend. Even if you take six months, this single skill of yours can give you financial freedom for life. Now is your chance to become The Millionaire Messenger and make millions while serving millions.

$$$$$$$

PROFITS

How much money are you leaving on the table?

When my batch-mates finished their Engineering in June 1995 (I finished six months later ☺), many of them got placed with companies like CMC Limited, TCS, Wipro, Infosys, and Satyam at an average salary of Rs. 7000-10000 per month. All of them were placed outside Delhi.

One of my batch-mates Siddharth got placed with CMC Ltd. in Ahmedabad on a package of Rs. 9000 per month. During a small visit to Delhi (his hometown), he popped in to my office (at that time, I was working part-time with a CAT-Prep company as a Sales Executive, Content Developer, and Assistant Faculty).

Siddharth: "I am not sure I can work at CMC for long. How do they expect me to survive on 9K a month?"

Me: "You mean too much month remains at the end of the money?"

Siddharth (laughing): "Exactly!"

Me: "So, how much do you wanna make?"

Siddharth: "30K. Imagine a thousand rupees a day! Someday I wanna make 30K a month."

(Ironically, I was making close to 40K per month – almost 500% more than Siddharth – in my part-time job, mostly because of my sales-commissions. And as you now know, I had been an utter failure throughout my engineering by every standard of imagination).

Me: "30K a month doesn't excite me at all."

Siddharth: "Ya, right! So what do you wanna make? One crore per day?"

Me: "Yes! At least I have the audacity to dream as much."

Food for thought: You can't ever outperform your self-image. If you put a small value on yourself, the world will never increase the price.

In all humility, I can say that I haven't still reached that level. The highest I have gone on to raise is Rs. 1 crore in two days. So only half of my dream is realized as of now.

How much we human beings are a slave to our own minds! If Siddharth (who was more talented than I was) had thought that he could make Rs. 1 crore per day, I am sure his entire life's reality would have been different. Siddharth met me again in 2011. And he kept on whining about his salary. He was working with an IT company in Bangalore for a package of Rs. 18 lakh per annum. I was again shocked by what he was earning.

I asked: "Don't mind me saying this but how come you are still at 18 lakh? I guess with your kind of experience, you should have progressed to at least 50 lakh."

Siddharth: "I find it disgusting to be at this salary, but what can I do? This is what the norm is across India."

"This is what the norm is across India" – *Outrageous*! How can someone else decide what you earn? And if 18 lakh is the norm, it is someone else's standard. In the book *Radical Careering*, Sally Hogshead makes a point that has since stuck with me. She says:

> "Refuse to settle for someone else's average. Reject mediocrity. Average is your archenemy. Traditional corporate culture induces mind-numbing homogeneity. Screw rational! Murder everyone's darlings."

I hate the word *average*. I just hate it. I hate all its synonyms (mediocre, norm, standard, defined, rational, just about right, decent etc.) too. 18 lakh may be the average Indian salary for most people at Siddharth's level, but why accept that average? Why accept that norm? Why accept that 'standard' salary? Why can't we raise our standard? To me the word 'average' implies: "Everyone has been considered."

If you don't set a baseline standard for what you'll accept in life, it will be easy to slip into behaviors and attitudes or a quality of life that's far below what you deserve. Don't follow the standard that the world sets for you. Raise your internal standard. And you can indeed raise your standard because

"Nature's Law of Averages doesn't apply to money or growth."

Let's understand this further. What's the average height of an adult in the world? Let's say 5′6″. What's the height of the tallest person in the world? Let's say the figure is 8 feet.

What is the difference between the two? Well, it is about 45%. Let's say, 50% for all practical purposes. This is Nature's law of averages.

Also, what's the average increase in height per year? And what's the maximum observed increase in height in a single year for any child above 10? I am sure it won't be more than 100% (double).

Now consider this: What's the average (per capita) income of all the adults in India? Let's say, $4000 per year. What's the income of the richest person in India? WELL! It is definitely not just 50% above $4000. A few billion dollars is going to be more like it.

Also, what's the maximum possible increase in someone's income in a span of just one year? Well, one of my students went from a salary of Rs. 6 lakh to Rs. 6 crore – a million dollars – in a single year. That's 100 times the original.

Watch her video here: https://www.youtube.com/watch?v=fD9ytx6C4CE

I ask you a question whose answer has to be AYEEEEEEEE!!!!!

How about giving yourself a 1000% pay-hike (10 times extra) in the next 12 months?

The saddest reality of most people in India is: We follow the strategy of the masses (bottom 99% people) and expect to become millionaires (the top-one-percent people). One of the most useful quotes that I have read in my entire life has been:

"Success leaves clues." – Tony Robbins

This is my personal translation of this quote: "If you want to be rich soon, copy a rich bloke's traits."

Looks quite simple, right? But whom was Siddharth comparing himself to? All his colleagues! When it comes to hopping jobs, most people in India are very happy with just a 30-50% hike. Why not emulate the traits of someone who, from almost nowhere, went on to become a dollar-millionaire—in just a year?

Over to You

What should be your game plan?

Start with this idea: "In the next 12 months, I want to earn at least four times my current income by spending one-fourth of the time." That's practically equal to 16 times your current hourly income – a straight 1500% jump.

Assuming you want to earn Rs. 1 crore at the end of the next 12 months, let's see the exact steps in The Solopreneur Blueprint that will take you there.

Passion + Purpose: Zero in on just one passionate idea that you think lies at the intersection of these four elements: passion, skills, impact, and money. Claim that topic. Announce it to the world. Start blogging about it. Say shocking things. Make a small video and use shock as a weapon. Let people know you are doing something like this. Get a website (preferably .com)/blog/YouTube channel and start posting your content. Also, capture your leads and start building a mailing list.

Personal Journey: Craft your personal journey in such a way that it automatically positions you as an expert in the topic you have chosen. Offer to speak free at some events. The idea is to get an audience somewhere so that you can record yourself live as you deliver your story. Follow a storytelling formula to tell your story; don't just shoot from the hip.

Perspectives: You can't develop your perspectives in a zillion disciplines in a very small amount of time. So the best step here is to be really specific. Get hold of similar products from the best experts in the world and study each of them absolutely effectively. Start an in-depth reading of your topic. This will be an ongoing process.

Product: Once you have the perspectives, create your UBS using a visual, acronym, alliteration, and numbered-steps models. While designing, always imagine how you will explain it to a 10-year old. Also decide how you would like to offer it in your one-hour sales session, in your book, in your two-day workshop etc.

Publish your content: Write a book around your idea (it can be done in less than a month). Also, publish all the content (whatever is possible as of now) that was discussed in the chapter on *Publishing*. Don't be shy of telling people whatever you are doing. Again, publishing a book may be easy but don't write a sloppy book that people will put down after reading just the first page. Follow a book-writing formula.

NEXT: Train 20-30 people free of cost in a single-day session. Collect their video testimonials.

Positioning: Although in the original Blueprint, this step comes before Publishing, I am taking it after Publishing as you will have positioned yourself somewhat by now. Now is the time to show your extreme rebellion to the world. Divide. Polarize. Shock. Claim the positioning The ONLY_____EXPERT in ______.

By this time, your website should be live and running.

Promoting (use Emails + Social Media): Use all of the above to your advantage and offer a 2-day workshop for Rs. 20,000 or more (don't charge less). If you do all that I have asked you to do, at least 50 people will surely register.

Preparing your CONTENT + Presenting: This is the real deal. If you can pull your first workshop off like a charm, like a dream, like nobody's business, YOU ARE IN BUSINESS.

The backbone of your workshop will be the novelty of the content, the usefulness and applicability of the content, engagement, humor, delivery, and your skills of Professional Speaking. Don't mess up this bit. **These 2 days will decide everything.**

If you pull this off well, you will make Rs. 10 lakh in 2 days. And, more importantly, you will have the chance to get the most raving video testimonials possible from people.

This step is so crucial that you need all the skills of Professional Presenting. Take care of the following:

- You must tell them at least 20 absolutely insanely novel perspectives.
- You must include at least 20 absolutely insanely engaging stories. All your stories must follow a formula.
- Your content must follow a very tight structure—to the extent that their attention is not diverted even for a moment. This is the most important point. Your content is everything. Don't mess up on this criterion.
- You must use humor throughout your 2-day presentation.
- You must ensure absolutely engaging delivery for these 2 days.

- You must come across as an absolute authority on your topic.
- Make sure you follow the principles of Professional Speaking, not Public Speaking.

If you pull these 2 days off really well, you are set to make your-first-million-dollars soon.

Next, promote a big event. If you receive the kind of feedback that I have received in the past, you can plan your next workshop for 500 people. Imagine this: if 500 people attend your 2-day workshop at Rs. 20,000 each, you can make Rs. 1 crore in just 2 days.

Next: Record this live event and create your video products. Price them at a minimum of Rs. 20,000 for every 6 hours of video. In the worst case scenario, if you sell just 10 sets a month, you will have Rs. 2 lakh per month in revenue (with more than 90% profits) without moving a single muscle. If you do really well, there is absolutely no limit to your growth.

If you play your cards right, your events are bound to be popular. Imagine doing just one 2-day event each month in different cities of this country. At these events, you may also sell your book + video products. With your book + events + video sales, you may reach a million dollars with just 12 such events. And I am not even counting your B2B engagements. You may exploit Corporate Speaking as a very lucrative option because business will start coming to you automatically.

Now imagine this: If your current income is Rs. 10 lakh a year, and, in the worst case scenario, you can make Rs. 1 crore per year by using The Solopreneur Blueprint, do you even realize how much money you are leaving on the table for others?

The minimum net difference = Rs. 90 lakh per year. This difference can reach Rs. 18 crores in the next 20 years.

The best case scenario: If you were to make a million dollars in your first year, over 10 years this difference can swell to Rs. 50 crore.

And you will be your own boss, love what you do, impact people, be a role model for thousands of people, and have loads of free time.

Do you still want to remain stuck in your current life?

$$$$$$$$

AS YOU PLAN TO JUMP OUT OF YOUR CHAIR

Are you a Bumblebee?

In June 2013, I was interviewed by the magazine 'Perfect Professional' for its July 2013 issue. The article was named *'Are You Failing to Learn or Learning to Fail?'* The interviewer, Luna Daniel, asked me a lot of questions about success and failure. As this is definitely not a book on motivation, I will steer clear of the discussion about failure. I am not enamored by failure. I am definitely a student of success.

I also don't subscribe to the rah-rah spiritual definitions of success. To me success is a game you play, alive and kicking.

So what Precisely is Success?

At the broadest level, success can be summarized in just three words: A.C.T.—Attraction, Contrast, and Trust.

Attraction: As a businessperson, you want to *attract* more customers. As a job-seeker, you want to *attract* the attention of the interviewer. As a startup, you want to *attract* the VC. As a speaker, you want to *attract* more listeners. As an author, you want to *attract* more readers. On a blind date, you want to *attract* your partner. So, the starting point of success is *attraction*. No *attraction* equals no success.

But in practical terms, *attraction* doesn't guarantee success. A baby's smile can also be *attractive*, but in practical terms you can't call it successful. What if your client finds the products/services of three more companies equally *attractive*? So once you have their *attraction*, the next condition is *contrast*. How are you different? How do you stand out? Why should they select you and not others?

But *attraction* and *contrast* can't win the day for you unless topped up by *trust*.

So, success can be summarized in just three words: *attraction*, *contrast*, and *trust*. Whenever you offer yourself (or your solutions) to the world, make sure you score 100% on all three. People will open their hearts and wallets for you.

Where is your Moon?

"The quality of your life is the quality of your communication."
– Tony Robbins

What a powerful idea! And I don't take communication to mean only how we talk to others. For me, the bigger part of communication is what we tell ourselves.

This is the communication I mean. I have seen it happen. The power of internal dialog is extremely strong. When I saw other professional speakers in other parts of the world, I just told myself (internal dialog) that I had to be on a global speaking stage. And I got there – in less than 8 months. Henry Ford summed it up correctly when he said: "Whether you think you can, or you think you can't, you are right."

Let's hear from the biggest cheerleader of it all: here's a man who led the United States of America to swing bigger than it had ever imagined—and, in doing so, broke the boundaries of all that we ever knew:

"We choose to go to the moon. We choose to go to the moon in this decade and do the other things, not because they are easy, but because they are hard, because that goal will serve to organize and measure the best of our energies and skills, because that challenge is one that we are willing to accept, one we are unwilling to postpone, and one which we intend to win, and the others, too. To be sure, all this costs us all a good deal of money. ... Space expenditures will soon rise some more ... for we have given this program a high national priority—even though I realize that this is in some measure an act of faith and vision, for we do not now know what benefits await us. But if I were to say, my fellow citizens, that we shall send to the moon, 240,000 miles away from the control station in Houston, a giant rocket more than 300 feet tall, the length of this football field, made of new metal alloys, some of which have not yet been invented, capable of standing heat and stresses several times more than have ever been experienced, fitted together with a precision better than the finest watch, carrying all the equipment needed for propulsion, guidance, control, communications, food and survival, on an untried mission, to an unknown celestial body, and then return it safely to earth, reentering the atmosphere at speeds of over 25,000 miles per hour, causing heat about half that of the temperature of the sun—almost as hot as it is here today—and do all this, and do it right, and do it first before this decade is out—then we must be bold. Many years ago the great British explorer George Mallory, who was to die on Mount Everest, was asked why he wanted to climb it. He said, "Because it is there." Well, space is there, and we're going to climb it, and the moon and the planets are there, and new hopes for knowledge and peace are there. And, therefore, as we set sail we ask God's blessing on the most hazardous and dangerous and greatest adventure on which man has ever embarked."

—President John F. Kennedy, September 12, 1962

You want to change your life? Be bold once again. Find your **moon**. Chase something so big and exciting that it's unimaginable to you and those around you. Be brave enough to take action, test things out—this is the stuff of courage, and the only approach to change that will fuel your engine and help your life truly lift off.

Change your peer group. The world is full of bitter, complaining, finger-pointing energy vampires who suck all the joy and ambition out of life. If you are like most people, you may be having negative, ambition-sucking friends whom you should have dumped years ago. All those people who judge, criticize, and make you feel terrible need to be thrown out of your life. On a scale of one to ten, how much do your close friends consistently encourage you to chase your dreams? How often do these close friends provide you with insight, information, and inspiration that challenge you to be a better person?

Think about this: If you are always at the top of the class, you are most probably in the wrong class. My rule is simple. When I dreamt of being successful, I surrounded myself with only those people who were already self-made dollar-millionaires. If I didn't find them in the real world, I bought their products, read their books, and attended their events.

Imagine wasting 6 hours of an evening with just booze, music, and absolutely mindless swinging versus sitting for six hours with someone whom you can have an extraordinary conversation with, learn something superb, challenge yourself, stretch your mind, laugh, and think. Both will help you unwind. But one will be forgotten even before the hangover is over; the other will add something to your existence forever. So, be bold and dump useless people from your life.

DECIDE TO ACT

"It is in your moments of decision that your destiny is shaped."
—Tony Robbins

Remember: Nobody gets it right the first time itself. You may be hit down on the floor, on the canvas. But the canvas is no place for the champion. The champion rises from the canvas and gets back in the game. Because champions are not born, they are shaped by endless practice.

Did you know: for many years, scientists thought (as per the laws of aerodynamics), the bumblebee couldn't fly. But it defies all rules and it flies. Successfully!

Screw the rules. You can FLY. Just jump off.

If you act upon the lessons in this book, I promise you that your **Purpose**, **Passion**, and **Profits** will MERGE.

What are you waiting for?

PROGRAMS BY SANDEEP GUPTA

Live Trainings and Video Products

All the programs run by me have a singular approach: ***The Solopreneur Life:*** More money, more time, more autonomy, and more impact.

Know The World In 24 Hours: This program is about developing such novel perspectives that you can constructively talk/debate with almost anyone in the world on dozens of topics. The topics include the most fascinating account of the inextricably intermeshed global geopolitical equations of the last 100 years, the remaking of capitalism in the aftermath of all the global economic crises, the world economy and all the twists in the global tale in the last century, the most scintillating account of evolution and the human brain, human domination of the planet, the shape of things to come, the psychological side of capital-markets and investing ... and a zillion other perspectives. You won't be able to find anything else even one-hundredth as valuable and jaw-dropping.

N.E.U.R.O.-Seduction: This is one of the two programs (the other being Tri-Summit Storytelling System) for which I am regularly offered $10,000 per hour by many of the companies abroad. I find this the most exciting idea for life-success. I doubt anything can be even remotely as fascinating as this concept. Combining the principles of Evolution and Brain Science, this session demystifies the science of persuasion like nothing else.

The Jet-Set Speaker

This is the program that, along with Tri-Summit Storytelling System, prepares you for a world stage, a stage where you are paid thousands of dollars per hour for speaking, a stage that enables you to sell your products from stage, and a stage that propels you into the Ivy-League of Speaking. This 50-hour program is the most comprehensive program on Professional Speaking anywhere in the world. The feedback for this course has been the best among all of my courses. Here are the six components of this course:

- **Stress Free Speaker S.Y.S.T.E.M.:** Imagine pacing back-and-forth and having racing pulses, sweating palms, pounding heart, tensing muscles, and wringing hands just as you start speaking. In other words, you are doomed. Being stress-free is the first, most basic requirement for you if you ever contemplate speaking. This six-step program goes in-depth into the on-stage-psychology of a stressed-out speaker and teaches you unheard-of tools to remain absolutely stress-free on stage.

- **Kick-S.T.A.R.T. Content Creator:** This program has been rated as the most useful among all my programs; it offers you such a tight-knit structure to write your books/draft your speeches that people will not find even a single boring moment in your content. By using ideas such as Salting/Selling, Teaching, Anchoring, Relating, and Takeaway/Technique, the content you deliver will be able to engage your listeners for up to fifty hours ... spread over five days.

- **Own The Stage:** The name says it all, I suppose. This program deals with how to come across as an absolutely unquestioned authority on stage without being detached or distant, and how to speak for impact, not for impression. I find it to be the most essential attribute for any speaker who wishes to change beliefs for his/her audience.

- **Dynamic Delivery Devices:** As the name suggests, this program is for alive, kicking, and impassioned delivery on stage. No matter how good your content, without awe-inspiring delivery it is like a body without the heart/soul. This program discusses ten advanced tools for an out-of-the-top-drawer Delivery.

- **The 5C's of Engagement:** If you can't engage your audience, you are dead meat. This program discusses all the tools needed to make sure that you don't lose your audience even for a second. They will be there, leaning and hanging on your each word, no matter how many days you wish to speak to/train them.
- **The Laughter Lever:** If you can't make people laugh, you shouldn't speak for more than a few minutes. This program teaches you some principles of comedy that you can incorporate in your speeches so that your speeches are never, ever boring. The day you deliver a boring speech, your speaking career will be over, at least with that (unfortunate) audience. You may not be out-loud-funny but unless there are lighter moments in your speeches, the audience is bound to tune out. This program will enable you to strategically place humor throughout your speeches.

Life Without A Boss

- **The Passion-Profit Matchmaker:** This session discusses my seven-step formula that helps you choose the right business for yourself.
- **The I.M.P.A.C.T. Work Equation:** This session focuses on a six-step model that helps you live the IMPACT life.
- **India's Only Solopreneurs' Club:** This is the monthly one-day meeting of Solopreneurs/Potential Solopreneurs. This is a very vibrant community of people you can learn from. This program is offered only LIVE.
- **B.O.L.D. – Beware Of Lady Dynamites:** The most sensational session for women Solopreneurs around the world; the program

is filled with an absolutely practical toolkit for ambitious and bold women who want to break free, celebrate themselves, and live their bliss.

Tri-Summit Storytelling System

Stories are the currency of human contact. Nothing positions you better in the eyes of the client that your own story. But storytelling is not just random art; it is fire + formula, art + algebra. To completely mesmerize your audience, your story needs to follow a formula, a structure. This program teaches you the storytelling structure in the grandest detail that anything can ... anywhere in the world.

- A breathtaking 10-Step formula to writing kickass stories for your books, websites, and blogs.
- An incredible 25-Step formula to delivering an absolutely power-packed punch by electrifying storytelling on stage.
- **India's Only Corporate Storytellers' Club:**
  - **For C-Level Executives (individual training)**: If you are a dynamic organization-leader craving to tap the power of persuasive storytelling to make your speeches come alive and to fire people up, you can't get anything better on this planet. Post this program, you will start inspire people like TED-presenters. This program is exclusively for the CXO Club, not for everyone.

C.Y.U.B.S. – *Creating Your Unique Branded Solution*: This turbo-charged, exercises-driven session helps you come up with your framework, your model, your UBS. The session on UBS is topped up by a session on how to create your live, video, and online products.

Universal Attraction Triggers: This absolutely insane, one-of-a-kind program nails the science and art of attraction by using an unheard-of concept called seven Universal Attraction Triggers. After attending this program, you won't remain the same; your life will change forever. This is the surefire mantra to big-ticket successes.

You will learn the art of crafting such compelling messages that people will surely open their hearts and wallets for you.

A.P.P.E.A.L. – *Adorable Personal Positioning Exuded All Life:* as we have discussed throughout the book, the importance of Personal Positioning can't be overemphasized. Positioning is 90% of the Solopreneur game. This practical, exercises-driven session totally nails the unmistakably intriguing world of Personal Positioning. By the time you walk out of the doors, you will be ready to charm the world.

Your First Book: This program covers all the aspects of writing (story, structure, content, and flow), editing, publishing, and marketing your book (fiction/nonfiction/self-help/autobiographical message, or what have you) ... from scratch to finish. This is the only such program in India (I am the only author in India who trains you to be a bestselling author). This program also covers other types of contents that you need to publish: Videos, Websites, and Collaterals.

Pitch and grow rich chronometer: This program addresses a very specific topic: making a huge amount of profits by selling your products from stage. What should your 60-90 minute speech include so that people run to the back of the room to buy your stuff? My 60-minute Speech Chronometer (clock) gives you a minute-by-minute structure of such a Sales Speech, a speech that enables you to make thousands upon thousands of dollars in just one hour. This program is offered as the final frontier in the Million-Dollar Solopreneur Blueprint. If you master this, you can just do a few Sales events in a year and you will be able to pocket a million dollars, without moving any extra muscle.